ADVENTURES

WITH

INDIANS AND GAME

ADVENTURES

WITH

INDIANS AND GAME

TWENTY YEARS IN THE ROCKY MOUNTAINS

BY

DR. WILLIAM A. ALLEN

Skyhorse Publishing

First Skyhorse Publishing edition 2016

Skyhorse Publishing books may be purchased in bulk at special discounts for sales promotion, corporate gifts, fund-raising, or educational purposes. Special editions can also be created to specifications. For details, contact the Special Sales Department, Skyhorse Publishing, 307 West 36th Street, 11th Floor, New York, NY 10018 or info@skyhorsepublishing.com.

Skyhorse® and Skyhorse Publishing® are registered trademarks of Skyhorse Publishing, Inc.®, a Delaware corporation.

Visit our website at www.skyhorsepublishing.com.

10 9 8 7 6 5 4 3 2 1

Library of Congress Cataloging-in-Publication Data is available on file.

Cover design by Richard Rossiter

Print ISBN: 978-1-63450-439-3
Ebook ISBN: 978-1-5107-0030-7

Printed in the United States of America

DEDICATION.

INTRODUCTION.

This fascinating narrative, which the publishers experience much pleasure in offering to the public, has come forth as the result of years of loving participation in hunt, in Indian fighting, and in nature studies, by Dr. W. A. Allen, a typical oldtime Westerner, who, for over a quarter of a century, has taken part in the wild life of the West, being in the early days the trusted leader of immigration, a keen enjoyer of the sports of the chase, a crack rifle shot, who won and successfully maintained an enviable record as an Indian fighter of bravery and distinction.

This volume will be welcomed by lovers of nature and nature studies for its scientific value in the portrayal of natural history; by the "old-timers" of Montana and Wyoming for its lifelike retrospect of the days when every man held his life in his own hand, and peril lurked on the bank of every stream, glanced out from every mountain side and lay in wait everywhere amid the rich grasses of the plains; by all lovers of their country, true Americans, for the light it throws upon the flora and fauna of the primitive prairies and mountains, and for its minute descriptions of the different animals that were once the occupants of this then strange, mysterious, unknown country, since that time wrested from savage domination for the establishment of civilization by that class of tireless, brave and heroic pioneers, of which the author is a notable example.

An attempt to narrate, even in epitome, the incidents which have characterized the life of this Montana pioneer would transcend by far the normal province of an introduction, yet it would be culpable neglect were there failure to advert to their more salient expressions, for he stands prominent, not merely in a local way as one of the founders of the city of Billings, Montana, but also as a leading student of physical, natural and geologic history, and as an acknowledged authority on the flora and fauna of the Rocky Mountain region. He is known as a "dead shot" hunter, and such journals as the Turf, Field and Farm esteem him as a valuable correspondent and contributor to their columns.

Descending from good old English and Irish families of the long ago, Dr. William A. Allen is far more proud of his relationship on the paternal side with Ethan Allen, the "hero of Ticonderoga," and on the maternal, with the distinguished Benjamin Franklin. He was born at Summerfield, Noble county, Ohio, on September 2, 1848. His finishing literary education came to him in an Ohio normal school, and, showing marked mechanical tastes, he early became both a blacksmith and a maker of guns. In 1877 he started for the Black Hills. At Spearfish, now in South Dakota, he joined an emigrant party of 250 persons, here commencing his twenty-five years of adventurous western existence and hunting exploits.

Starting for Bozeman, in far off Montana, the strenuous

existence of the frontier soon came to the party in full vigor in attacks of savage Sioux Indians, in which a number of the company were killed and others wounded, Doctor Allen being among the latter. Returning to Spearfish to reform their organization, Doctor Allen was made the commander of the train, which he divided into four companies. Their route took them up the Belle Fouche River, past old Fort Reno, through Wyoming, by the site of Buffalo and old Fort Kearney, thence up Goose Creek, where, in a spiteful attack by Indians, one man was killed and others wounded.

In the locality of the historic last battleground of the gallant General Custer, they remained three days, which they profitably passed in a careful study of the grounds, tracing accurately the various movements of the contesting foes until they ended at the pile of bones that showed where the last white survivors met their death. Here the party divided, one part going to the Crow agency, another by Pryor's Pass, Sage Creek and Stinking Water crossing to Wind River, the others, with Doctor Allen, going to Camp Brown and to Bozeman, the end of their journey.

Various vocations have been followed by Doctor Allen in the Great West. He was for some time a blacksmith, having a shop at Bozeman, later an express messenger, the government blacksmith at Fort Custer, a stockraiser on Canyon Creek, in 1882 removing to Billings, then a mere cluster of crude, primitive dwellings, where he erected the first house in the Yellowstone Valley covered with a shingle roof. After this he thoroughly pursued the study of dentistry in the Chicago College of Dentistry and in Haskell's Post-Graduate School of Dentistry, and has since maintained his home dental office at Billings, acquiring an extended reputation as an expert in both mechanical and surgical branches of dentistry. The genial Doctor is a true "old-timer," a man of honesty and integrity, charitable and generous to his fellow men. He has ever been a total abstainer from intoxicating liquors. Honored as a citizen, reverenced as a pioneer, few people of the state of his adoption stand higher in the estimation of the public.

We have closely adhered to the plain vernacular used by the Doctor and trust that the reader will fully appreciate the thrilling interest of the narrative. Of the numerous illustrations, so profusely scattered through the work, too much cannot be said of their accuracy and value. Many are from photographs taken by Doctor Allen himself, in localities and under circumstances never again to be repeated. The Past of the Great West here comes once again to the reader, in all of its romance, peril and enjoyment, and, in the perusal of these pages, the greatly changed and practical Present will be for the time forgotten.

PREFACE.

As I look back after many years spent on the plains, mountains and rivers of the Northwest, the trail seems long and full of dangers of every description. Many personal accidents, hazardous undertakings, conflicts with savages and wild beasts in a strange land, loom up large as I recall my past days. I can see the trail running through fifty years, from childhood's day, and, in that time, the Great West has undergone many changes. I have witnessed the extermination of the buffalo, the wild horse, the fan-tailed deer and the wild pigeon. The elk, the moose, the caribou and the antelope families are now reduced to a few scattering bands, occupying only the very wildest and most inaccessible places, far from the haunts of man. I wonder what the next fifty years will bring forth. Deer parks and game preserves will no doubt be the order of the day. The youth will read of the buffalo chase and of the wild Sioux and will earnestly wish that he could see these strange, exciting phases of a life which has even now passed away forever.

It has been my lot to see many marvelous sights and my fortune to be a part of not a few strange episodes. I have seen millions of buffaloes extending in a mass as far as the eye could see on plain and mountain. It would require three days for these herds to pass a given point. The Sioux Indians, the Cheyennes, the Crows, the Blackfoots, the Bloods, the Flatheads and many other tribes have passed away before my eyes. The wild scalp-dances are a thing of the past, and the sun-dance, with its tortures as a test of endurance, is now only a memory. This record of my life is neither wholly comprehensive nor consecutive. I have recorded only those events, truly within the scope of this book.

We can look back to the great Missouri and see no railroad crossing it until 1882. The opening of this wonderful thoroughfare through the Dakotas and Montana, made access to the wealth of the Northwest comparatively easy. The face of the earth then speedily changed. The old hunter, and the trapper with his packs and traps, stole sorrowfully away to new fields in virgin hills, far from civilization, where they now reside or have passed with feeble footsteps over the Great Divide. Next came the era of the plow. The pastures of the buffalo were planted in grain and civilized homes were built. The plains were irrigated and fertilized and now they blossom as the rose.

My life on the plains has exposed me to all kinds of inclement weather, but, at the age of fifty-three years, I am still in perfect health. I attribute this condition to the fact that I use no alcohol, drugs or narcotics in any form, nourishing myself with plenty of fresh air, pure water and wholesome food. My sight is as good as ever, and I can still travel over rugged heights with younger men.

Go into the mountains, study the trees and flowers, explore the canyons, smell the fragrant hemlocks and pines. Consider the ways of the majestic eagle, the noble elk, the cunning fox and the practical beaver. Learn of the flowers and ferns which beautify the hills, whose veins of gold, copper and iron will enrich generations yet to be. Through these creations, study the great Creator, and you will be the better because you will feel the greatness of the Maker, and realize your own insignificance without His guidance.

W. A. ALLEN.

TABLE OF CONTENTS.

ILLUSTRATIONS.

MONUMENT ON CUSTER'S LAST BATTLEFIELD.

CHAPTER I.

I am impelled to write of my adventures in the far West, and of the many strange and thrilling incidents through which I have passed, but my thoughts recur with persistent obstinacy to my childhood, so I will give a brief retrospect of those early events which did much to shape the course of my subsequent days.

My father died when I was two years of age, and from this time my childhood days were spent at the farm of my uncle, Samuel Guiler, near Freedom, Noble county, Ohio. My uncle was a Christian, unwisely generous and a true sportsman. Hence it is that I was imbued with the spirit of sportsmanship. But, had it not been for my innate love for the gun, I never would have become proficient in its use in the small amount of time allotted to such sport in farm life. My first killing was a chipmunk when I was seven years old. That event is still photographed on my memory, as clearly as is the bright spring morning down in the corn-field, where the red bird and chipmunk were then in part-nership in harvesting the newly planted corn.

As the years passed, I began my rambles through the forests, with my mother as guide, for she was in constant fear when I was out of her sight. On one occasion I stole out alone with my old Kentucky rifle and soon found a large gray squirrel culling nuts in a hickory tree. With the tread of a cat I soon located him and prepared the limb of a dog-wood tree for a rest. When the stinging report broke the stillness of that grand old forest, centuries old, down came my prize. With a joyful heart I took the trophy home. My people were delighted and I was then privileged to tramp the forests at my will. I was devoted to that old gun, and, as the days went by, I became a marksman of no small skill. For the amusement of my boy friends I would shoot the clapper out of a cowbell at forty yards distance, or could cut off a pig's tail with a rifle ball as though with a knife.

In 1864 my mother remarried and moved to Centerville, Iowa. Here I soon became noted for my daring and mark-manship. Presently I became acquainted with the city gun-smith, and, after showing him some of my feats with the rifle, he accepted me as an apprentice. I worked with a will at my new trade, for I was devoted to anything pertaining to a gun. After a few months I undertook to make myself a gun, every part of which should be my work. I set my tapered barrel in the guide and commenced my labor of love. As the rifles were cut, one by one, and the trimmings placed, I could see that a gun was being formed and was pleased beyond words. After three weeks we went to the testing field. Judge of my surprise when my instructor, with my rifle, drove seven balls into a stump four hundred yards away. I was now, in my own estimation, a man, ready to stake my life on the accuracy of that gun.

An expedition was then about to start for the Rocky Mountain country, and I was acquainted with the organizer, whom I had met several times while making rifles for the expedition. I decided to join him and his party, and was outfitting myself as rapidly as my means would permit, when my stepfather, in terms which admitted of no misunderstanding, informed me that I should not go. I rebelled at this, and, as I had never received much encouragement at his hands, I resolved to leave home for all time.

I collected my scanty wardrobe and prepared to go to the home of my uncle in Ohio. With a sorrowful heart my mother met me at the gate, and while our tears fell like rain, she kissed me good-bye and placed a little Bible in my hands, exacting a promise that I would ever refrain from liquor and gambling. I readily gave her my word of honor, not thinking seriously of its importance, but in after years I have had frequent occasion to recall her words. The little Bible has remained in my possession, a comfort and a link to the past. It has survived two fires where the houses were burned to the ground, and passed through a flood where it floated for twenty-four hours. The lessons learned from the little book still have a sacred place in my heart.

With my relatives and friends in my old home, I soon forgot the unpleasant scenes I had left behind. I remained in this place for several years. During this time I met and married a Miss Houston. My salary as a farm hand was very small, and I engaged in blacksmithing with a partner, whom, six months later, I bought out and started business for myself. By this time I was the father of two boys, and as I looked into their bright little faces, I would ask my wife if we would ever be able to educate them as we wished to do, for we were very ambitious for them. Doubting our ability to do this in the overcrowded East, for their sakes I resolved to take my chances of fortune in the wild, unbroken country of the West. I had counted the cost of hardship and danger, of death, but was undaunted. Stories of gold fields in the Black Hills reached my ears, and I determined to depart thither. When my intention became known, I was overwhelmed with all kinds of advice, admonition and warning, and as the days passed the excitement became more intense. But my hopes were strong and I was a healthy man, accustomed to a hard life.

On the 12th day of March, 1877, I set out for the Black Hills. At Zanesville I met Alexandrer Mitten and Thomas Sipe, of Sarahsville, Ohio, who were also bound for my destination. We joined company and journeyed to Sidney, Nebraska. As we arrived at this frontier town, the rain was falling in torrents and the Black Hills stage came in with a dead driver in the boot, shot by the Sioux Indians. While this circumstance did not enhance the cheerfulness of the situation, neither did it deter us from proceeding.

On the following morning we contracted with three men, who were driving teams to the hills, to take us as passengers. Our baggage, consisting of seamless sacks, was brought forward and weighed, and we soon struck a bargain for the transportation. As soon as our train had pulled out, we saw a band of Pawnee Indians, and Mitten predicted that our "hair would be raised" before we reached the hills. After we had travelled about ten miles, we were informed that the teams were exhausted and that we would be obliged to walk the balance of the day or return to Sidney. In the trail of teams better fitted than ours, we walked through rain and mud, and snow, not only that day, but all of the succeeding days until we reached the hills.

Our entire trip was one of hardship, danger and privation. Our bedding became wet and our nights were often spent shivering with the cold. Often our attention was called to the bodies of men killed by Indians. They were those of hunters and trappers who had lost their lives in this huntsman's paradise, and no one took the trouble to bury them. The remnants of burned wagons, pack saddles and camp kettles were to be seen at almost every crossing.

When we reached Deadwood, we secured shelter at fifty cents each in a small stable. We slept there rather comfortably. On the following morning we went to the postoffice and took our positions behind a line of men half-a-mile long, who were waiting for mail, and in our turn at the window we received our first letters from home. After a few days in Deadwood, we went to False Bottom and started mining, after providing a grubstake including sugar at one dollar per pound, evaporated potatoes at one dollar per pound, bacon at one dollar per pound and flour at fifty dollars per fifty pounds.

While the boys were getting the camp started, tents erected and the cooking utensils ready, I shouldered my rifle and started for the woods. A fine rain was falling. I went to the southern ridge, started in my hunt down among dead timber, where after about a mile's travel I came to a blacktail sign. While I was carefully scanning every tree and bush I saw a large pair of ears rise from a bed of moss under a large pine tree. I could not see the body to which they belonged, but I thought that at one dollar per pound they represented sufficient value to bring me one hundred dollars. I aimed at the neck beneath and fired.

Instantly a beautiful doe started down the ridge at a terrific speed. I threw in another shell as quickly as possible, and as she bounded away I shot her in the back. She proved to be a prize, and I soon had the skin off the fore-quarters. I cut off the saddles and started for camp. My comrades hailed me with delight and we soon had a feast of venison. Two of the boys brought in the remainder of the deer, and I made a rug of the skin, which proved to be very useful in my after travel.

We prospected this creek and found extremely fine gold dust but no pay dirt. Our provisions were decreasing and we had very little money left. Meantime I sharpened miners' tools until I had earned enough money to fit us out again. When word came that gold had been struck in rich deposits on Wind River in Montana, as miners are always ready to "stampede" on short notice, we went thither with the crowd, taking with us a year's provisions.

SITTING BULL.

War-Chief of the Sioux.

CHAPTER II.

Spearfish was our objective point, and, with a party consisting of thirty miners, we pulled out of False Bottom over a road which never had been worked. We arrived at Deadwood Corral, halted in a little valley, where we struck a camp and began our preparations for the great trip across the plains. Our attention was presently attracted by the rapid firing of rifles, and we soon saw that a party of whites below us in the valley was fighting for life, against great odds, with Sioux Indians. Curling smoke could be seen and we knew the prairie had been set on fire. Some of our party started to the rescue as fast as their horses could bear them, but were too late to aid.

Seven men and one woman had been massacred. They had not only been shot and scalped, but their ears and noses had been cut off, and they were otherwise mutilated beyond recognition. Powder had been shot into their faces until all possible chance of identification was lost. The bodies were hauled into camp in a small cart, the bed of which was not long enough to hold them. Their limbs hung down and dangled to and fro as the vehicle moved. It was a horrible sight. I vowed that I would be one to follow that trail of blood until we had avenged the death of these emigrants. One after another, with blanched, but set faces, we put down our names on a paper, until twenty had volunteered to avenge the innocent people who had met such a fearful death. It was a determined party that left our camp. The trail of blood was two hours old, but our horses were in good condition and we sped down the valley of death. We came soon to the dreadful field of carnage. The wagon had been burned, the horses killed and the harnesses cut to pieces. The ground was covered with clothes and stained with blood from the innocent sufferers.

The Indians' trail led off in the direction of lower Red Water and Hay Creek, and on this track we started at a swift gallop. After a few miles of silent travel, we passed through a wooded canyon. Here the Indians had watered their ponies and left a few articles of no value. We dismounted and held a short council while the horses drank from the rivulet. We decided to follow and surprise the savages at their camp for the night. We selected two of our lightest riders to skirt the stream and the eastern and western hills, in order to get the course they were traveling. The remainder of our party kept the trail, which we followed at a rapid gait.

About twelve o'clock our west side man signalled from a butte. We were soon at his side and in plain view of a small band of Indians. From the direction from which they came we could not determine them to be the band of assassins whom we were trailing. However, they quartered on the same creek which we were following and, as they disappeared over the steep bank, we started in pursuit. On nearing the water, the Indians must have heard the thunder of our horses' hoofs as we rode swiftly down the valley, for they came out on the same side they had entered, about one hundred yards below us. We at once sent a volley of bullets, and two Indians swung out of their saddles. Like a flash the Indians started for a green forest far down the valley, with our party in swift pursuit. Our repeaters were making the valley ring and we saw another warrior writhing in death. But at this point the Indians swung into a rough ravine and disappeared.

We followed a short distance and found blood on the trail, whether this was from horse or rider we could not determine, but, for our own safety, we returned and scalped the three Indians, who were laden with plunder from emigrant trains. Flour and sugar were found on one warrior. We soon started once more in pursuit of those who had escaped us. After traveling about ten miles we found the trail very fresh. Water carried on to the bank by the feet of the horses was not yet dry. We held a short council, then sent out scouts with field-glasses to search for the savages. At sundown they returned, having located about thirty Indians in a camp in a small basin in the valley of the Red Water. We drew as near their camp as possible, avoiding all chances of being discovered. We ate a lunch and then Thomas Nickelson and myself started to make a survey. It being moonlight we soon located the camp, where the savages were already in motion. Their camp fires still smouldered. We followed them about a mile further to the place where they went into camp for the night. This camp-moving is an old trick of the Indians to deceive their enemies and to induce them to make a charge on an abandoned camp. Having once more assured ourselves of their location, we crept softly away and soon rejoined our comrades.

We planned to "cache" our horses, leave five good men with them, while fifteen went to attack the camp. We knew, however, that we should be compelled to exercise continual vigilance.   John Wustun, Thomas Nickelson and myself were detailed to overlook the ground and make the final arrangements for the attack.   Each man, with a magazine rifle and a belt full of cartridges, crawled up to within fifty yards of the camp.   We found the Indians in the mouth of a deep, narrow canyon, their horses above them in the canyon, which made it impossible for the animals to get out without passing over their masters' beds.   They had some fine war-horses, with Pintos and sorrels which showed good blood, but all were firmly hobbled and picketed.

Believing that we had secured the best possible location, Nickelson, being very light of foot, went after the other boys.   The Indians were cooking and not a word could be heard.   The fires, made of buffalo chips, whose flame resembles that of charcoal, were blinded as much as possible. After the savages had finished their supper I expected to see a scalp dance; but in this I was disappointed, for they no doubt felt it more prudent to wait until their return home, when all, old and young, male and female, might mingle in the jollity, while the sounds of the tomtom would keep time to the fiendish actions and the "Hey, hey, a hey, hey, a hey!" so curdling to the blood of a white person.

I could plainly see the goods taken from the emigrant's wagon, and the sight made me run my hand along the barrel of my rifle to clear all obstacles and push a cartridge carefully home.   I knew it would not be long until they would begin to look after their horses and prepare to sleep.   We occupied the point just over the canyon on the south, where we held the party of Indians in full view, although we could not see them as well as we desired, for they glided around stealthily, sometimes appearing in the shadows like wild animals.   Our party soon came up eager for the attack.   One gaunt warrior started in the direction of the horses with a bundle of something which I took for bedding; as he passed a blazing fire Thomas Nickelson sent a bullet through his brutal heart.   Fifteen rifles rang out simultaneously.   Fire flew and horses plunged headlong through camp, while volley after volley was sent after the Indians.   It was sometime before they got out of our range and a deadly fire was kept up until they reached the north side, where they began to return our fire.   When one of their rifles flashed we sent fifteen bullets after it.   I do not think two shots came from the same spot.   I received a wound in the foot, and Nickelson's arm was shot through the fleshy part near the shoulder.   Wustun had his hat-rim cut off by a bullet which made a terrific noise.   We could hear the Sioux tearing through the bushes and dry leaves, but they were soon past our range, and we hastened back to camp on another branch of the creek.   We then placed onr horses on good feed, for on the following day we had a long ride before us.   After stationing guards, we lay down to rest.   Thus closed one of the hardest day's work of my life.

We awoke at the gray of morning and our men were soon ready to resume their journey.   After a breakfast of salt pork and dried buffalo meat, we examined the battlefield.   Several men stood guard on the bluff, while the remainder searched every foot of ground in the vicinity.   The bodies of eleven Indians and fifteen horses were discovered.   It was not strange that some scalps were taken, for our watchword was "Vengeance."   We followed the trail a short distance.   It lead away from Spearfish, and, as we were already in the midst of a savage tribe, with no provisions and tired horses, we left this desolate spot and started for Spearfish.   We knew that some of Uncle Sam's wards would not return to the agency for their rations on the next issue-day.   These were the petted warriors under Sitting Bull, Rain-in-the-Face, and Gaul, who were stationed at Red Cloud Agency, and by a lenient government permitted to ride the plains and murder emigrants.

At Spearfish we were to rejoin our main party, which was there in camp. We started across a country looking beautiful with the advent of spring. The rich grass was matted on the earth and pine trees dotted the landscape. Parks were numerous and the antelopes roamed over a thousand hills, while the huge buffaloes in great herds wandered carelessly about, scarcely noticing our presence. We made a hard ride and reached Spearfish about dark, for we had lost the route and had gone out of our way. As we passed up the valley we were surprised to see a white woman riding toward us at full gallop and leading a pack. We suspected that it was "Calamity Jane" and pulled up as she approached.

"How! How!" said she, "Where are you fellows going?" "To Spearfish," we answered. "Well, you had better get to Red Water Crossing, because there is a party there corraled by Indians, and there are some women in the bunch. I would go with you, boys, but I have this dispatch to take to Custer City. Take that trail and follow my tracks and you are all right." Nickelson declared that he must go to Spearfish to get a fresh horse, and would follow and meet us at daybreak. John Wustun and Grizzly Bill offered to go with him. We arranged our plans to meet at dawn, for we knew that there would be trouble.

Calamity Jane was a noted female scout of the western frontier from 1870, her daring intrepidity, her rapidity of movement and her deadly skill with firearms, as well as the qualities she displayed as a rider, causing the Indians to consider her as possessed of supernatural powers. She was given her doleful name in 1872, by Captain Egan, then commander of the U. S. army post at Goose Creek, whose life she saved. The captain was shot in an Indian fight and was in danger of death, when the brave female scout appeared on her horse, shot the Indian nearest the captain, and, picking up the wounded and unconscious officer, she placed him in front of her on the horse and carried him to the fort, uninjured by the shots of the other hostiles. When Captain Egan learned of his rescue, he said to his preserver: "You are a good person to have around in time of calamity, and I now christen you Calamity Jane, the heroine of the plains."

Col. W. I. Cody (Buffalo Bill) tells this story, which I give to illustrate the character of this brave woman, who did so much for the safety of the whites in pioneer days. She was only fitted for a wild and adventurous life and closed her eyes in death in the summer of 1903.

"In 1876 this daring woman by a most courageous action saved the lives of six passengers on a stagecoach traveling from Deadwood, S. D., to Wild Birch, in the Black Hills country. The stage was surrounded by Indians, and the driver, Jack McCaul, was wounded by an arrow. Although the other six passengers were men, not one of them had nerve enough to take the ribbons. Seeing the situation, Jane mounted the driver's seat without a moment's hesitation, and brought the stage safely and in good time to Wild Birch. Jack McCaul afterward recovered, and some time later, while in Deadwood, he assassinated Wild Bill, one of Calamity Jane's best friends. The murder was a cold-blooded one, and it was the general opinion that lynching was only too mild for him. Calamity Jane was in the lead of the lynching party, and it was she who captured the desperado. She had left her rifle at home, but with a butcher's cleaver she held him up, and a very few minutes later McCaul's body was swinging from a cottonwood tree and his soul had passed over the great divide."

We rode into camp, where the story of the eleven dead Indians was not referred to, for we well knew that there were several persons who would go no further if the truth was told. Red Water Crossing was twenty miles away and we knew that it would be necessary to rest, procure something to eat and have our wounds dressed before doing anything else. I cut my boot from my foot, washed and dressed the wound, replacing the boot with a Sioux moccasin.

After supper we secured twenty recruits and started at twelve o'clock for Red Water. This was a hard ride and several times I fell asleep in the saddle. But we pressed on and at last found ourselves in the breaks of the river. The red hills of this country resemble those of the limestone hills found in the East and Southwest. We were now on dangerous ground, as our camp was at the Crossing and Indians were on every side, therefore no time was to be lost. The birds were chirping for the dawn and the wooded fringe of the creek began to become discernible as we passed on in silence. Coyotes were prowling around and their chorus was almost as blood-curdling as the song of the Sioux scalp-dancers.

We beheld at this point a blue smoke curling upward, close to the valley through which we were riding, and we felt sure that this must indicate the presence of the party we were to meet. By peering closely I could see Nickelson in the uncertain light, eating what later proved to be buffalo steak. We approached the fire and were heartily welcomed. Nickelson came forward with a blessing and assured us that we were none too soon. Our horses, not being needed for the present, were put with the rest of the animals and a strong guard set around them. We were soon eating, and I shall ever remember with gratification the buffalo marrow-bones and the bread which Mr. Nickelson had prepared for us. Our time was precious, but we ate heartily.

Presently Tom drew me aside and said he had something to show me. We went behind the wagon where he pointed out to me the bullet holes made in the attack of the day before. He said that the Indians had been signalling in the early part of the night, and that his wife maintained that they had been reinforced since dark. From the manner they had made the attack yesterday on the knoll across the creek, he said he had learned there was only one break where they could get down; that we would command that place and at the same time protect the camp. It was fast growing gray and we knew that very soon we would be the probable subjects of attack. Every sign of our horses and of every person was securely hidden, in order to give the impression that we were unprepared. We "cached" twenty of our men opposite the mouth of the break to await results. The remaining men were stationed to protect the camp and horses.

The chirps of the early songsters were now heard, and the eastern horizon began to illuminate the plains stretching toward Centennial Prairie and Red Canyon. All of us were impatient; some were murmuring about the wet grass; others decided that no attack could be made. The time wore on and the great calm which precedes a storm enveloped us. Not a leaf stirred. The wolves had skulked away with the coming of day. At last I thought I could hear the rumbling of footsteps. Soon there was no doubt about the sound, which came nearer, clearer than before. "Let every man be ready and do not fire until you see the color of their eyes," said Nickelson.

Just at this moment a yell broke on the air and the brow of the hill was covered with warriors, each one striving to outstrip his comrades, leaning forward on his war horse. Our boys lay flat in the grass, as silent as death. The unearthly yells pierced our very hearts and when the Indians were within seventy yards of us, Thomas Randall, of Chicago, sent the first ball from his Remington rifle 45,105. This was followed by nineteen deadly bullets of all sizes.

We sprang to our feet in a cloud of blue smoke, and, as we all had repeaters, there was one blaze of fire. Horses were rolling down upon us, and the report of rifles was deafening. One Indian who had determined to die on the field, or who could not manage his horse, rushed toward Nickelson and myself. He was nude and his hair was streaming in the air. Our two rifles crashed and he fell forward, but raised again and fired a carbine at my face. Fortunately for me, I was only powder-burned, and he fell to the earth.

The Indians were gone as quickly as they came. The smoke cleared away and around us lay fourteen Sioux warriors, five dead horses and three with broken legs. These we shot. We held a council and decided that if the news of this affair should reach the Red Cloud Agency we would be speedily annihilated by overwhelming numbers of Sioux. A deep washout was near at hand, so horses and Indians were dumped in and covered with bushes and old dead sage. Passing on our way we soon found two trappers and their burned wagons. From Red Canyon to Centennial Prairie and Pumpkin Buttes half-burned bones and wagons, dead horses and camp requirements were strewed about where scores of men had yielded up their lives to the deadly attacks of the Sioux and the Cheyennes.

We felt that the best thing for us to do was to return to Spearfish, and there organize a strong train, which should be well armed, or give up the trip, so dangerous with lurking foes at every point. Our plan of operations we voted

to keep secret, and, as far as possible, was to be concealed
from the entire train, for we well knew that the women
would all refuse to proceed if the worst were known. From
now on the utmost secrecy was to be practiced and all of our
night rides were to be attributed to the prospecting for gold
and mining fields.

We returned to camp, partook of a splendid breakfast
and immediately set out for Spearfish, where we met our
friends and were given a warm welcome. The remainder
of the day was spent in organizing for the trip to the Big
Horn country. Two hundred and fifty people were gathered
by the time our party returned. But the memory of those
who had been killed gave an unfortunate aspect to affairs,
for when we mustered all who would go, we numbered only
one hundred and fifty persons, with only fifty-six wagons.
Enough for a good company, if all would stand together.

CHAPTER III.

We started once more for Red Water Crossing, led by Colonel Beard, of Nebraska, a brave, unselfish man, a splendid looking fellow, six feet three inches in height. At this crossing a part of our train had a short skirmish with Indians, and five of our men were killed. The country was all alive with the savages. Each day brought us news of fresh massacres. We stayed at the crossing one day to discuss and decide upon the best means of checkmating the enemy, who threatened to be a terrible peril to us. A dispute arose among the men, and, as some would not listen to reason, Colonel Beard resigned the command. One after another was selected to fill the vacancy, but all shrank from the responsibility. Death lurked on every hand. Some of our own men, by reason of their insubordination, threatened to become troublesome. The situation was a perilous one, any one assuming charge of the train would have a great responsibility on his shoulders.

At this point John Wustun mounted an old wagon and called the attention of the crowd. "We are in a dangerous country," he said, " and there are twenty men here who have tested the ability of a certain man in this company to lead this train to its destination. We have tried him on Red Water and on Hay Creek, and I move that W. A. Allen be elected by this train as general, to have full control, each member bearing his part of what ever befalls."

The vote was taken and was almost unanimous in my favor, women also were allowed to vote. I arose, thanked the members of the party for the honor, told them I would willingly share the fate of my brave comrades, but that there were old plainsmen in the company, one of whom, I felt, should have the honor conferred upon him. Besides this, I had no suitable horse on which to look after the duties of a company such as ours. Thomas Nickelson led forward a superb saddle-horse and said that it was mine for the trip. Thus the matter ended and work began.

In our party two secret organizations existed, both of which I knew. One was designed to look after Indians and to deal with them according to the standard of the West. The other was an organized band of horse thieves. This last organization was the more difficult to watch, but, as I had taken place in command, I intended to control these masters so long as I acted in the capacity of leader. Organization and discipline were the two principles which must be enforced to the letter.

My first move was to cut our train into four divisions, the first one, captained by John Wustun, of Chicago, a general favorite, and a man already tried and found to be staunch and trustworthy. The second division was placed under Captain J. Patton, of Sioux City. Mr. Patton was a shrewd person, keen of observation, always jolly, who understood his men well. Hiram Bishoff, who was placed in charge of the third division, was brave and courageous, always watchful of his trust. Division four was a splendid lot of fellows, whose captain was Samuel Houston, of Texas, a grizzly bear in the fight, always ready with his old Hawkins rifle, which never left his side.

Our train now started without a hitch, and we had little pack-outfit, led by Charles Blackburn, the poet scout. When we made our first camp I received some instructions in camping from Nickelson. At his suggestion, fifty-six wagons formed a corral by putting the tongue of each on the inner side and the front wheel inside of the hind wheel of the forward wagon, thus making a deadlock not easily moved. Thus our stock was enclosed, and, early the following morning, while the outfit was preparing to start, I gave an order for the guards to shoot any person seen inside of the corral after the retiring hour. In this way our horse thieves were checkmated and they never secured the stock which they sought. I then started off for a moment to take a view of the surrounding country. I saw five large buttes, which raised their heads like sentinels, overlooking the verdant valley, which is about one mile in width and is a good grazing district. Red Water takes its name from the color of the earth through which it flows.

A hard day's drive brought us to the headwaters of the Red Water. We settled our camp in a beautiful spot surrounded by high hills. There was plenty of wood and pure cold water at hand. After the heat and toil of the day it seemed a little paradise. We felt all of that sweet comfort and content that the weary man of business feels, when, in dressing-gown and slippers, he throws himself into an easychair before the cheerful fire, to rest from his day's labor. The camp had the appearance of a theater, where all were eagerly performing their respective parts.

Suddenly the music of a violin and a guitar, touched by skillful fingers, broke upon the stillness of the evening.

All conversation was suspended. The music and quiet were in perfect harmony with the scene around us. The most hardened men among us were touched and soothed. Women and children wandered aimlessly over the carpet of buffalo bunch-grass, drinking in the sweet melody. Some of our men saw smoke curling through the air, and reported two Indian camps not far off. We put out a double guard for the night and rested securely. Our route, as far as we could see, now lay over a fertile country, covered with vegetation.

We soon found out that things were not as they had looked from a distance; here and there were barren tracts. While passing through a small district, covered with scrub oak, four white-tail deer (cervus Virginianus) came bounding through the bushes. Several shots were sent after them. All was excitement. They came closer and closer until they were within two hundred yards, when I drew my 45-60 Winchester, took aim at a large buck and missed him entirely. I made a second trial and broke his hind leg. Down he came, but gathered himself up again and went hobbling off into a ravine, dense with oak. A young man followed and shot him through the head. We had a good supper of venison and lingered over it for about two hours. We spent the remainder of the evening having a good, social time, visiting and becoming better acquainted with one another.

We made the acquaintance of all the ladies: Mrs. Marble and her daughters, Ella and Mollie; Mrs. Reed, who kept the homesick and discouraged ones roaring with laughter in spite of themselves; anyone determined to have the blues had to shun her society; Mrs. Nickelson, who was braving frontier life with her husband; Mrs. Chamberlain and her little daughter, who was a great pet with all; Mrs. Burnstein, who was in company with her husband, and Mrs.

Lyons.   Among the men were lawyers, doctors, dentists, carpenters, blacksmiths, shoemakers—all kind of professional men and mechanics.   We had also two traveling saloons, cows, chickens, and everything necessary to establish a first-class colony.

We were climbing a high hill, overlooking a vast country.   With our field-glasses we saw, about ten miles off, a small party of Indians, loaded with plunder.   I longed to get hold of them and relieve them of their burdens, but it would have been folly to try to overtake them, so we moved leisurely upward, mounting higher and higher, until we landed on Belle Fourche Heights, which we chose to call Mt. Zion.   Here is a wonderful lookout.   With the aid of our glasses from this elevation we sighted the great Sugar-Loaf monument, standing clear and white in the sunshine. Our pleasurable excitement was still further augmented when we beheld, for the first time, the snow-capped peaks of the grand old Rockies.   From boyhood I had looked forward to this moment.   I had longed passionately for a glimpse of these mountains and of the game that inhabits their fastnesses.   I had read and heard much of them, and vowed to myself that when I became a man I would visit them.

Now that I really beheld them, though a long way off, I could not withdraw my gaze. As the sun poured down its fiery rays, the snow upon their summits gleamed like great diamonds.   Off to the northwest lay the gliding Belle Fourche, twisting and writhing like a serpent in its winding bed; the current was almost stopped with innumerable beaver dams.   On the north the rimrock stretched far away, shelves of sand rock projecting far out over the stream, which is thickly fringed with spruce and hemlock.   I stood lost in contemplation of the scene, when a voice behind me asked, "Are you in a trance?" I turned and Miss Marble stood beside me. She reminded me that it was time for the evening repast, and invited me to sup with her family. I was glad to once more partake of food prepared by experienced hands. The table fairly groaned with good things—warm biscuits, maple syrup, fried venison and other dainties that we, who had not our wives with us, had not tasted for a long time.

At this point upon Mt. Zion some of the men declared their intention of pulling out by themselves, saying they would not travel so slowly; that they could easily make thirty miles a day, while we were making from twenty to twenty-five. This was the first trouble that we had had among ourselves since leaving Red Water. I determined to put a stop to it at once, and for good. My position was a trying one at best, and I would not be annoyed by complaints all along the road. We were traveling as fast as the endurance of our horses would permit. It would not be prudent to wear them out with the greater part of the journey still before us.

I said nothing until we were ready to break camp in the morning. I then called the attention of the grumblers, and told them I knew of the threats that had been made and would now give one half-hour for all who were dissatisfied to pull out, but that all who left us now, positively should not join us at any future time. The half-hour passed. No one had made a move. In this way the dispute was settled and we heard no more of it during the trip.

That morning I left Wustun in charge and galloped on ahead to reconnoiter and, if possible, to bring in some game. I drove the spurs in Charlie's flanks and started him into a swift lope down a deep cut canyon. I soon encountered abrupt rocks, almost impossible to pass, and was obliged to slacken my speed. I urged Charlie onward with voice and spurs; the noble animal escaped with but few scratches. Going up the deep cut in the hill, the tracks of a large bear attracted my attention, but it was impossible to follow them. When I had gone about five miles the canyon became fearfully dark and deep; the place presented an unearthly aspect. Here and there a large bird would rise, flap its wings and fly slowly up the gorge. My horse was worn out and would not go without repeated urging. The overhanging rocks, the tall green pines, the damp atmosphere filled me with a sort of supernatural dread.

The large, vulture-like birds kept circling around overhead, causing a shudder to pass over me. I made every endeavor to find a way out of this loathsome den. I found a mountain-sheep trail winding among the rocks, over brush and fallen trees, which I followed until I came to a perpendicular rock five feet high. It seemed utterly impossible to scale this rock with my horse, but I determined to make a trial rather than retrace my way. My good horse tried to make the leap, but fell back. I think he was as anxious as myself to escape from the canyon. I took a long picket-rope from my saddle, climbed to the top of the rock by holding on to shrubs, passed the rope around a large pine tree, and, with the end in my hand, made my way below. I gave Charlie a tap with a stick, and, when he made a leap,I pulled with all my might upon the rope that was fastened to him. To my joy, I landed him on the rock and was not long in joining him.

I found myself on a high plateau. Vegetation was alive. Bunch grass and wild oats were here growing in abundance. Deer tracks and sheep signs were to be seen all around. I took a survey of the country while Charlie got square with the oats. I was at least ten miles from camp, in one of the worst Indian countries along the route. I might be attacked by Indians at any moment, and, tired as were both my horse and myself, we would stand a poor chance of escaping. I started out to rejoin the train. A distance of about five miles brought me into a barren region, covered with sagebrush and alkali. This is one of the peculiarities of a mountainous country—here and there a strip of fertile soil, sometimes covered with beautiful flowers, surrounded by barren earth, like an oasis in the desert.

It required all of my powers of persuasion to induce my horse to struggle through this dense undergrowth. While crossing a little ravine, I saw a large doe standing about one hundred yards off, on a shelf of rock just above a precipice twenty feet high. I drew my rifle, fired quickly and did not touch a hair. Disgusted with myself, I dismounted, threw in another cartridge, drew a hard bead for her heart and shot. She bounded over the ledge and disappeared. I took a look for Indians, tied Charlie to a tree, and prepared to follow her. There was no way to do this but to climb down a fir-tree, and it was beyond my reach. By placing one end of a small log on the ledge and the other in the forks of the tree I was enabled to make the descent. The doe lay close to the ledge. She had made but one leap, shot through the heart. I lost no time in securing the hams, strapped them to my saddle and pushed on.

When I reached the first coulee, I found fresh pony tracks. Much distressed in mind, I followed them, for I guessed from their direction, that savages were following our train, and did not know what might have happened during my absence. I soon saw a party of the miscreants in camp, on the side of a hill. I took a peep at them through my glasses. While watching their actions there appeared to be, all at once, a great commotion. They started to their

feet, seized their guns and commenced shooting just over
the ridge. A few shots were returned. I guessed that they
were firing at some of our men, for their actions did not indicate that they were after game. Unseen by them, I gave
them a volley of five well-directed shots. At that moment
Grizzly Bill (as we had nicknamed him) came dashing
past on his little charger, like a bird on the wing. He alone
had borne the fire of the enemy. I did not stop to see what
effect my shots had had, but their cries told that some of the
bullets had not missed their mark. They discontinued the
fray, dragging their effects out of sight.

Night was now coming on apace. I had been wandering around since early morn, and was still some distance
from home, for which I made a bee line, directed by the
smoke of the campfires. When I arrived there I found that
I had been given up for dead. Mitten felt sure that I had
been scalped by Indians, and was thinking how he had best
break the news to my family. He had long before prophe-
sied that my recklessness would sooner or later lead me to
my death. After eating a lonely meal, for it was long past
the supper hour, I felt as well as ever.

Just as we were starting out in the morning, a white-
tail fawn as spotted as a leopard crossed the road in front
of us. "Now for a race, Charlie!" I said, and away we went
over sagebrush, prickly-pears and fallen logs, but soon overtook it, as its hind leg was broken. It looked so meek and
cried so piteously that I hardly had the heart to kill it; but
meat we must have, and I quickly dispatched it. Several of
the boys were in an engagement with sagehens, and I joined
in the sport. Altogether we killed a number. We then
dressed them and skinned the fawn.

"Allen," said one of the boys, pointing to a large covey
of grouse (bonasa umbellus) "we will give you a test." I

had said that with my Winchester I could kill two at least out of five of these birds on the wing. My first shot brought down two as they slowly arose and flew away from me.

"That won't do, it was a chance shot; you must try it again," said the boys.

I tried again and brought down three. Colonel Warner, with his breech-loader, brought down two more. The grouse started up about twenty paces from us and were slow on the wind, but I scarcely ever failed to bring down two. Such a dinner as we sat down to that day! We fairly reveled in luxuries. Grouse, venison bacon, potatoes, syrup, flapjacks, with coffee strong enough to speak for itself. We stopped eating when there was nothing more to eat. Our motto was, "Eat as long as you can see anything to eat; never lay by anything for tomorrow." We had a novel way of washing our dishes. Each man filled his pan about half full of sand and with a bunch of grass rubbed away until it was bright and clean. All were thus washed, thrown into the mess-chest and put away.

At Antelope Springs we stopped to examine some coal. The vein was from five to ten feet deep and seemed to be very good. The country around this point is covered with sagebrush. This brush grows about three feet high on the open ground, spreads out in every direction and is very stiff and unwieldy. Mingled with this were prickly-pears, making travel very toilsome. This day the teams showed unusual signs of fatigue; some of the horses staggered like drunken men. The mules and the oxen stood the trip much better. We were now in sight of Powder River. Just as the first teams were driven into its waters up jumped a five-pronged buck. Several shots were fired, one striking him in the front leg. As he swam towards the rear division, another volley was poured into him. We exchanged congratulations on the feast in store for us.

Next day, August sixth, we laid up on the banks of Powder River to rest our worn-out teams, and to repair things generally.

After a good night's rest, we were ready for business. Like the busy bee, we improved the shining hours, repairing wagons, shoeing horses, mending harness, cleaning guns, binding up bruises, cleaning the mess-chest, patching clothes and the hundred-and-one things that must be attended to on a march like ours.

The banks of the Powder River are low and sandy. The sand is not of the ordinary kind, but is black, resembling gunpowder. Beavers were to be seen here in large numbers. At this point the redskins had burned two forts, the taking of which they accomplished by stratagem. They drove a large herd of buffaloes past the forts, and, while the soldiers were in pursuit of the game, the whole tribe made a rush upon the defenceless forts, set them on fire and killed a large number of the soldiers who rushed back to prevent their designs. Twenty-five miles off lay Crazy Woman's Creek, the next stream in our route, where we arrived early in the evening, tired and sore. We threw ourselves upon the bank and discussed what we should have for supper.

"Well, boys," said one, "Can't you smell fish in this stream?"

"If I was not afraid the fish commissioners would come along and catch us, I would get out my seine and take a tumble through these peaceful waves."

"Get the seine," shouted a dozen voices.

The seine was produced with much mock fear and trembling; half-a-dozen men plunged in, boots and all.

"Keep down the lead-line, boys."

"Raise the lead-line, we have a whale."

"Hold on, boys, I'm swamped."

In this way we amused ourselves while wading around. With one plunge we swept through a place where the water was three feet deep and stuck on a sandbar. We were amazed to find that we had about two bushels of white suckers. We had a regular jollification on getting to shore. We were now dividing the spoils. Some tried to get away with their arms full of live, wriggling fishes. Others held them by the tails. I had a better way. I filled my old white hat, which, with the rim turned down, held about half a bushel. Our mess had fresh fish for supper, and we did not mind the bones a bit. After we had eaten, we took another turn in the water. The fishing continued until it was dark. I believe the whole party had fish for breakfast. To celebrate our good luck, we gathered around the little stream and sang, "Shall we gather at the river?" Then followed a regular wardance, concluded by war-songs. No savage, with a dozen scalps hanging from his girdle, could have felt happier than did we, on that memorable night.

In the morning we resumed our journey in high spirits. Our mess paid a visit to George Silverberg and his comrades. We found George gloriously full. We sang all of the songs that we knew appropriate to the occasion, and left him unspeakably happy. We then sought out William Baldwin, and he sang for us, "The lousy miner." For the time we forgot all our hardships and thought only of present enjoyment and the gold-fields ahead. Our concert came to a close as the dinner hour approached. That evening we pitched our moving tents, one day's march nearer the Big Horn, near Clear Creek. Here we caught a few trout, and smiled at the idea of eating suckers. Oh! no. No one but a "tenderfoot" would eat suckers. The water of this creek is very clear. The bed is lined with boulders worn round and smooth by the swiftly flowing waters. The banks are well-defined gravel-beds. The grass is deep and luxuriant. From here westward the country is mountainous. During the day we saw antelopes and a white-tail deer, but they were too far off for a shot.

Our next camp was on Big Piny Creek, at old Fort Phil Kearney. The fort had been burned to the ground some time previously. Human skeletons, bleaching in the sun, told us a sad story of a heartless massacre. The fort was established in July, 1866. Forts Reno and Phil Kearney and old Fort Smith on the Big Horn were built to protect the overland trail and the miners who thronged this thoroughfare on their way to the gold fields of Montana. Near Fort Kearney, Colonel Fetterman and eighty-four soldiers were massacred by Indians. They were in the line of duty, covering the trail of wood-haulers, and guarding them from danger.

The massacre occurred on December twenty-first, 1866. No one was left to tell the sad story except the woodchoppers, who heard the firing. It seems that there was a lack of good scouts in this particular locality. About 1868, "Portugee" Phillips was the scout to carry the first news of Phil Kearney's massacre to the army officials at Fort Laramie, and they thereupon buried the brave boys. We stopped and made camp, to view the battlefield or rather the place of the massacre. The soldiers were passing to the north, when, ambushed by an overwhelming number of Sioux, they were shot down from a ravine filled with chokecherry brush and willows. As we passed the line of graves on the sharp ridge, now near the main traveled road from Sheridan to Buffalo, we were greatly impressed by the evidence of the savagery of the children of the plains; we were not less impressed by the generosity and bravery of the soldiers who had here laid down their lives to help blaze the trail for the millions who will hereafter travel this road of civilization.

As our train passed slowly along we neared the beautiful sparkling water of Goose Creek, and it was a glad sight to our eyes, tired and weary after three months of hard travel, danger and hardship. We were passing into what seemed to be a valley of beauty, profusely set with studs of green cottonwood, willows and mountain ash.

CHAPTER IV.

Our train halted on Middle Goose Creek, Wyoming.
We intended to camp here for a few days to rest our weary
animals and to prospect for gold. Presently we pulled out
to make a camp farther down the stream, and I left Thomas
Randall in charge while I took a ramble across the country.
To see our train strung out along the stream, as it wound
its way down a beautiful meadow, was truly a pleasing
sight. The creek abounded with delicious trout and white-
tail deer, antelopes and buffaloes sported in great numbers
on adjacent hills. Grouse, prairie chickens and sagehens
thrust themselves upon our notice. Nature had been spec-
ially lavish in this section, and the red man was not slow to
appreciate the fact. The Crows, the Cheyennes, the Sioux,
and the Shoshones were continually fighting for the mastery
and possession of this Eden of Wyoming.

My horse was eager to join the train; his large brown
eyes glistened and he pawed the ground while I saddled
him, adjusted my cartridge belt and thrust my old Bullard
rifle through the sling. As I raised into the saddle he
sprang forward. We headed for the mountains, and we flew
over the green meadow, rich in a thousand beautiful flowers, whose perfume filled the air and mingled with the spices
of red willows.

BEAVER CUTTING TIMBER.

Billy had measured off many miles when we came to a plum thicket, heavily loaded with red fruit. Out of this shot a bunch of white-tail deer and we gave chase. I checked our speed when we came to a steep gulch and sprang to the ground. As the deer went up the opposite side, I selected a young buck and fired, breaking his back. I dressed him, put him behind my saddle, and started on. Shortly after a large band of buffaloes (bison Americanus) were seen crossing some low foothills, coming toward me on the run. I suspected that Indians might be at their old trick to get our party after buffaloes, then swoop down on us and seize our stock, so I started for the train. I had not gone far when I saw the buffaloes pause to drink, after which they returned whence they had come. This relieved my mind, and I started to explore some large beaver (castor Canadensis) dams which I had seen from a foothill nestling among a grove of small cottonwood trees.

On nearing the valley, I crossed a trail forty feet wide. At first sight it looked like a well-traveled road, but, on closer scrutiny, it proved to be a beaver trail worn perfectly smooth. I dismounted, took off both deer and saddle, and picketed my horse in a secluded nook where he could get grass and water. Having made a careful observation of the surroundings, I found myself in one of the most extensive beaver colonies that I had ever seen.

The stream at this point was a series of little lakes, and, about one hundred yards below, I could hear the triphammer and piledriver thumping away as each beaver's tail came down on the new construction. I was soon near the dam, but could get no satisfactory point of observation. A few yards ahead of me stood a boxelder tree, and I began to crawl toward this as carefully as if I were stalking a band of deer. The bushes and willows covered my approach,

2

and presently I was among its branches. Carefully I peered from out its green foliage. What a sight met my gaze! Seventy or eighty beavers were working in broad daylight as though they feared none of God's creatures. I took a careful survey of the country for Indians, saw that my horse and gun were within easy reach and dismissed all fears. I was eager to give my entire attention to what I had often sought after but never had the pleasure of seeing until now.

The dam was nearly one hundred yards long, about six feet wide at the bottom, and narrowed to two feet at the top. It comprised stones, logs and willow branches, packed together so firmly that it was impossible to dislodge any portion of the structure. I first sought to divide the workmen according to their respective duties. The most prominent figure was that of an old beaver, gray with age and of enormous size, whose function seemed to be that of a general supervisor, for he sat apart on a small sandbar. My attention was next attracted to some very large, strong beavers, who placed in position material brought forward by others. I begrudged the occasional glances which I was compelled to give to satisfy me that no Indians were approaching. I was curious to know how those hod-carriers, who came forward with their tails loaded down with mortar, obtained their load. The mastermechanics with their tails beat this mortar into position. I peered a little farther over the boughs, and saw that down below the dam, close to the original creek bank, where some water was creeping forth, was the mortar trough. Some beavers were engaged in mixing this sticky clay and placing it on other beavers' tails, who in turn went straight to the dam with it.

I could scarcely remain silent when I saw this proceeding, for how this mud was moved had always been a mystery to me, as it takes tons of it to make a dam. I beheld with delight even the youngest beavers coming with long willow twigs in their mouths to lay beside the masters. These in turn took them, cut them in pieces and stuck them down by rearing upon their hind feet, holding the twigs fast in their teeth while pushing them firmly into the dam. As soon as the mortar was taken from the hod-carriers, it was stamped solidly into position by the tails of the workers.

Such precision and orderly work I have never seen carried out except by bees and the red ants of the plains. I noticed two or three times that the youngsters had a disposition to play between loads. The masters would then thrust out their necks and show their teeth; this never failed to cause a scamper back to work. In my delight and curiosity, I pressed far out on a small limb and suddenly it broke, letting me down noisily. The superintendent beaver, upon hearing the first sound, jumped into the water and gave one stroke of his tail which sounded all over the series of dams. Instantly every beaver had disappeared and dead silence reigned. My horse was still cutting the grass without fear or excitement, so I slid to the ground, took my belt knife, cut a stout stick, sharpened it and began to tear out the fresh work which was almost completed.

It was almost impossible to move any part of the masonry which was secured so firmly. But, after a hard struggle, I got the water started, and went back to my tree to await results. I was sure the beavers had not smelled me, and, such being the case, I was confident they would soon return to their work. Shortly I saw the old boss stick his nose out of the water and swim over to the dam, carefully scanning every object, and raising on his hind feet and sniffing all around. After satisfying his curiosity, he gave two terrible blows with his tail, then ran to where the water was pouring over the dam. He went through all manner of antics and was soon joined by the entire force.

Strange to say, no other beaver after coming to the surface, even stopped to look or sniff, but started to work as though he were a fireman at a fire, and in one-fourth of the time it had taken me to start the water, they had stopped it entirely. Now the regular work went on again without interruption until all parts of the dam were of uniform height. After a fearful beating of the surface with their tails, all of the animals jumped into the pond and began swimming as if in perfect delight. Then the old superintendent went all over the newly constructed dam, going last to the point just finished, which he gave a few pelts with his tail. He then joined the others in the swimming celebration. When I alighted from the tree, the customary alarm was given and all the beavers disappeared. I was soon on my horse wending my way to camp, and passed beaver dams until I had to leave the creek bottom and take the higher ground.

Years of careful study and close observation have convinced me that there are two species of beaver in this country, one having a larger inferior jaw, curving more than the other, with two double toenails on the inside of the front foot. This is contrary to the clasification of zoologists, who declare that the bank beaver, which builds in steep banks, differs from those who build houses of logs and brush. Beavers build as necessity compels. Where banks which do not overflow are available, they build there, but where such banks are not to be found, they build houses out of logs, interlined with brush daubed with mud.

Six beavers are able to roll a log one foot in diameter and eight feet long. They often cut cottonwood logs and carry them into water where there is a hole deep and still. When the log sinks from the weight of the absorbed water, it is secured firmly and in winter the bark is eaten from the log, the log is pulled out into the current and floats off.

I have seen cottonwood trees four feet in diameter

cut down by beavers. During such work the superintendent takes his stand, while the workmen, one after another, begin to gnaw around the tree. As many as can work comfortably at a time continue until the job is finished. When the tree is about to fall, the superintendent gives the signal and all run to the water. After the tree has fallen, another call is given and all proceed to cut limbs great and small. The precision with which they fell a tree, either to make a dam or turn a stream is wonderful.

Often for some unknown reason, a beaver will leave the colony, burrow a hole in a bank and live a regular hermit's life, having nothing to do with his fellows. These are called bachelor beavers by old trappers. A large beaver will weigh seventy pounds. The outer or guard hair is reddish and coarse, with a thick velvety fur underneath, which keeps the water away from the bodies. The female bears from two to six youngsters in the spring. These little fellows are very busy people, cutting and carrying everything that comes in their way. In point of instinct no animal is superior to the beaver. His feet adapt him to all kinds of building, the hind ones being webbed. This enables them to stand easily in soft mud, and gives them power in swimming. The fore feet have no webs, being designed for constructing dams and pushing sticks into the earth. The tail is flat and used as a trowel, a hod, and as a rudder.

We left this lovely valley which had afforded us such a rest and bountiful supply of game and fish, moving north. We bade farewell to Wyoming and its rich pastures, its buffaloes, elks and deer, and entered the cloud-capped reaches of Montana, whose clear, cold streams and majestic mountains, clothed in perpetual snows, stand out in bold relief against the azure sky. After a weary journey, we landed on the Little Horn River, and arranged for a three-days' rest on the last battlefield of the lamented Custer.

CHAPTER V.

On the morning of August 18th we were camped on
the Little Horn River, just opposite Custer's battlefield.
Our teams were exhausted after a long trip and we held
a council at which we decided to remain here long enough
to rest our weary animals. Our tents were soon pitched in
the valley where Sitting Bull and his warriors had camped.
Buffalo bones, elk heads and deer antlers were strewn over
the valley and along the river front, while the bent-willow
sweat-lodges were still standing, with the rounded pile of
small boulders, just as they had been left by the red man.
The earth still showed small trenches where the large, round
tepees had stood, and the stakes and picket pins were still
in the ground. After a careful survey of the valley we decided to cross the river and examine the battlefield.

On the seventh of June, 1876, General Crook had
struck Sitting Bull and put him to flight after a severe
thrashing. This so humiliated the Indian chief that he sent
runners to the Northern Cheyennes asking them to join
him at once on the Little Horn, whose waters were already
rising from melting snows.

His scouts had located General Custer at the mouth of

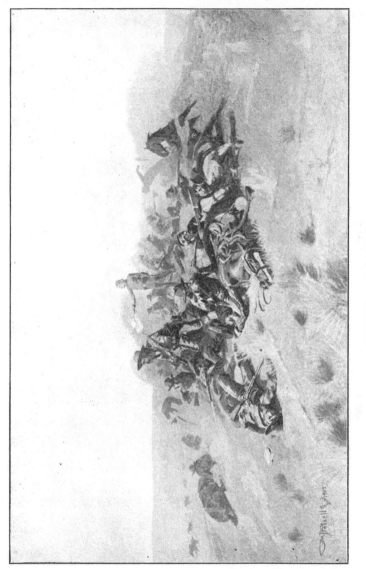

CUSTER'S LAST BATTLE.

the Rosebud on June 22, on their way to the Little Horn, and he immediately concentrated every available warrior to meet the yellow-haired chieftain.

Sitting Bull hated the paleface, hated civilization and its drudgery, and was eager to strike at any of its products and representatives. From his camp he sent out braves, across the plains and mountains, to notify his fellowchiefs that soldiers were coming to kill his people and destroy their property. Ghost dances were then kept up until the Sioux nation was almost crazy. Daily new arrivals poured in to the aid of Sitting Bull. Presently the river was fringed with tepees for a space of three miles. Here were the warriors of the Sioux, Cheyennes, Minne-Conjoues, Orgolies, Uncapapas, Bloods, Blackfeet and Flatheads, whose lodges numbered eighteen hundred, by actual count of J. H. Butler, of the 5th U. S. Infantry, who was serving under General Miles and was on the field shortly after the battle.

Generals Terry and Custer had been sent by the War Department to capture Sitting Bull and to bring him to Washington. The command halted at the mouth of the Rosebud, where it empties into the Yellowstone, and held a council. General Terry sent Custer forward with instructions to strike the Indian forces at a certain point, while he would attack them by way of the Big Horn at the same time, and follow up the Little Horn. As Custer crossed by land Terry suggested that Custer take cannon and Gatling guns, but he declined to do this, saying that it would not be necessary. On June twenty-fourth, by a forced march, Custer made twenty-eight miles and camped on the Rosebud, a tributary near the divide between Sitting Bull and himself. He reached the camp twenty-four hours before the appointed time, held a council with his scouts, Bob and Bill Jackson, who reported that the warriors of a large Indian village were hastily preparing for battle and thought there were not enough soldiers to encounter them. Custer told them to go back with the packtrain, which they did. Mitch Buoy also reported that it was the largest Indian village he had ever seen, being over four miles long and containing fully eighteen hundred lodges and about six thousand Indians, and he also declared that Custer had not half enough soldiers to fight them. Here General Custer gave him permission to go to the rear, which he refused to do, saying: "I will go in, but I will never come out," and, after discarding his hat, he tied a handkerchief around his head and said that he was ready for the battle.

General Custer called his men together and told them they had a hard fight ahead, but if each man would stand at his post they would be victorious. Custer was then twenty-four hours ahead of General Terry. He sent General Reno to attack the camp at the head of the creek and with the remainder of his command Custer himself struck the village at the lower end. Reno had crossed the river with part of his command when the Indians forced him back, killing many of his soldiers, and completely overpowered him. Reno recrossed the river, threw up breastworks and made a stand. At this point Gaul with all his warriors flanked Custer on the east, closing in on his rear, while the Cheyennes occupied the north dry-gulch and the Sioux came in along under the banks of the river, entirely surrounding the soldiers, killing the entire command on June 25, 1876. When General Terry arrived on the field twenty-four hours later, he found the soldiers all cold and stiff upon the battlefield, scalped and mutilated beyond recognition. Captain Renteen, who had been sent to remain with the pack train, fell in with Reno and tried to bury the soldiers, but found it a terrible undertaking and an impossible task. The command fell back to their boats on the Yellowstone, where they were joined by Generals Crook and Miles.

When our party gained the other side, a horrible sight met our eyes. Each soldier, who with Custer had sacrificed his life, yet lay where he had fallen on that ill-fated day. Each move that was then made could be read by us as from the page of an open book. As we surveyed the battlefield we saw where Custer had led his brave followers to the crossing of the Little Horn and where the first volley of leaden hail had swept into and across that doomed company from a threefold ambuscade. This had poured from the banks of the Little Horn on the south, where the main camp of the Sioux was located, down the river to where the Cheyennes filed along Dry Creek, crossed the hilltop that Custer had just descended, joining the right wing of the Sioux, which had but a little time before emerged from an adjoining coulee, thus forming one continuous dead line which so encircled the gallant soldiers that not a man escaped. We paused and counted the remains of seventy-six who fell to win Montana from the savage. Continuing, we came to the place where the survivors of the first attack had endeavored to regain the hill and escape by the route through which they had entered this death valley. Here lay the bodies of fifty or sixty men and horses.

In their vain attempt to escape by the way they had entered, the remnant of that brave command found themselves confronted by thousands of Cheyennes and Sioux, who had closed in on the hill and effectually cut off their retreat, leaving them no alternative but to return to the knoll where now stands Custer's monument, and there concentrate all of their remaining forces to make one desperate effort for life and liberty. Thousands of warriors pouring in a deadly fire from all sides soon so thinned their ranks that

only Custer and a pitifully small number survived. We then
came to the center of death where forty men and their
horses succumbed to a relentless foe, whose numbers were
six thousand. Although they had been surrounded on every side with a desperate enemy, possessing advantage of
ground, and having a concentrated fire pouring into their
decimated ranks, they yet fought like demons from behind
their dead horses until exterminated.

A little further on, I found a small wooden cross. On
this was a slip of paper containing the following: "Here
is where Custer fell." Other crosses told of Colonel Keogh,
Co. I, Seventh Cavalry; Wild, Co. I, Seventh Cavalry; J. J.
Crittenden, Lieutenant Twentieth Infantry; and Balzar Custer. Although General Reno was close at hand, and dis-
patches were sent to him from Custer by Muggins Taylor,
who took his life in his hand to serve his country and delivered the messages faithfully, and, although Reno signally
failed to assist Custer and was branded a coward, the very
nature of the valley and the bad-land hills, would indicate
the sheer impossibility of his help reaching the battlefield
in time to rescue the brave fellows on that ill-fated day.
We returned from the field sick at heart, but, after a restful
night we concluded to pass another day there, as many
points of interest had not been seen.

We started early, determined to make the rounds of the
dead line occupied by the enemy. On the edge of Dry Creek,
on the ridge and in the coulee, we found thousands of cartridge shells lying in piles, each pile showing clearly where
each warrior was situated. From these points almost the
whole battlefield could be seen, and the savages under cover
could pour in a deadly fire without exposing themselves.
We made the round of the entire firing line, finding empty
shells by the thousand, fifty calibre needle-guns, Henry rifles

WHERE CUSTER MADE HIS LAST STAND.

44, some Long Toms, Spencers, 56 calibre, Winchester 44-40. Bullets were also found that had not been shot, also round musket balls, buckshot, and some odd shells which I had never seen duplicated. In my collection I have several of these with the cross sticks which the Indians used to rest their guns upon when shooting.

After the firing line had been thoroughly examined, we returned to the scene of battle. Here we found the triangle of dead men showing three distinct movements under a terrific fire from three sides, each soldier lying just where he had fallen, each with a small amount of earth thrown over him, with his head protruding from one end of the grave and his feet from the other. One very noticeable feature presented itself to me, the boot tops had been cut from the dead. Their skulls in many instances had been crushed and shot with pistol bullets after being killed. Scalps had been taken and some of the clothing was removed. No bullets or shells of the enemy were found near that last stand, showing conclusively that the battle and the last stand were fought to a finish at some distance, as Rain-in-the-Face told me afterward.

We could hear in fancy the terrible war whoop from six thousand throats reverberating through the hills, and could see the mad rush of these fiends, the bloody scalps, and the ghoulish throng plundering the bodies of their fallen foe of every article of value, and their later triumphant return to the camp that extended for six miles along the banks of the Little Horn River. We could seem to hear the hoarse voice of Sitting Bull give orders to gather the dead Indian warriors and lay them to rest in their blankets. Then a funeral dirge is sung by the friends and relatives, and, as they are buried, according to Indian rites in trees and on the limbs of trees, a long last wail of lamentation, resembling the cry of wild animals, dies on the sighing winds. The mourners place themselves at the graves and remain apparently grief-stricken while the chiefs, Sitting Bull, Rain-in-the-Face and Gaul, hastily arrange the scalp pole upon which scalps are hung by the score.

The warriors speedily assemble, camp-fires are built, the tom-toms are brought forward and the great scalp-dance begins. Slowly the muffled sounds echo from valley to hill and from hill to valley. The wild war-notes from thousands of throats unite and the braves glide around like evil spirits. Old men with warclubs bound about like deer, strike the scalp poles, with bead-like eyes they renew their youth, while with fiendish delight they gloat over the stiffened forms of the pale faces. Intoxicated with victory over the race they hate, their fiendish delight knows no bounds. On they go, with tom-tom pealing, the muffled sound of thousands of moccasined feet stamping time to the blood-curdling music. Howling dogs take up the direful cries, which echo from river to plain, where the wolves repeat their echoes to the farther mountains.

It is pandemonium let loose. Devils chained a thousand years are now freed. As one set of dancers becomes exhausted and sinks to the earth, the gap is filled with another crowd, crying and wailing, the gestures of each set being more fierce than those of their predecessors. Gaudy feathers, war bonnets, paint and human blood bedeck their grim visages. Hags a century old are reeling around the death ring. Close at hand lie forty-two warriors silent in death, and the wails that come from the mourners sound like those of lost souls. Joy and sorrow mingle together on the Little Horn, whose placid stream glides by, crimsoned with both the blood of the red man and of the palefaces. The tom-toms subside until its muffled sound is almost extinct and the war-notes and dances of six thousand souls are hushed, while myriad camp-fires reflect fantastic images gliding to and fro like goblins.

The chieftains appear upon the scene, the signal for a deafening outburst. The field groans, the hills tremble, the assembled multitude pound the earth like war-horses approaching battle. Tepees are torn down, buffalo robes fly in the air, ponies pull their picket pins, consternation seizes the passion-drunk multitude. Some plunge into the river, while others fall to the earth. The squaws shriek with terror, the children huddle together in bunches. Warriors become insane, shooting their rifles and revolvers, brandishing their knives, flourishing their war-clubs. Night wears on and the braves one by one fall on the earth exhausted, until the chant is gradually ended, and all sink to slumber, except a few sentinels, who are posted lest some evil spirit swoop down and exterminate them all.

The horror of the slaughter seemed greater to us than we had before realized. That such a massacre was possible has been the wonder of all who have seen the battlefield. But to one who has been through the wilds, and who knows the cunning of the savages, there can be but one conclusion. The trail that Custer and his men followed was made by fully five hundred warriors of the Red Cloud, Sioux and Cheyenne tribes. Their trail was easy to follow, but the presence of the bands that came in from the north and west were not discovered until too late. Whether this was the fault of the scouts or whether the blame should be attributed to the officers will never be known, as those who were on the field will forever remain silent. There is no doubt that our army scouts have no superiors and that the art of trailing is primarily American. We find scouts among the mountains and on the plains, following the faintest of impressions. A stone removed, a blade of grass bent, is sufficient to guide them. The slightest indication is noted and followed as accurately as a bloodhound follows its scent.

These six thousand warriors had met in this valley from many trails leading through jungles, over mountains and across plains for the avowed purpose of exterminating "The Yellow-haired Chief." Sitting Bull and his followers had made the camp with this end in view, as there was one place only where the river might be crossed. The wily old chief knew that the soldiers must cross from the east to the west side, and that the valley where they occupied the ridge between the Little Horn and Rosebud rivers was well defined. They could easily watch the line of march and place their warriors contiguous to the ford by the time Custer arrived there. This was promptly done while the soldiers made the last two miles of their march. Never was a more strategic movement carried out than that last one against Custer. Swift and terrible was the execution. While the Indians were all under cover, the soldiers were in plain view and they were killed from every side.

The last forty or fifty men died among the bodies of the horses, which had been killed for breastworks of defense as a last resort. These heroes of the plains well knew what to expect at the hands of the savages, many of whom were then being fed, clothed and armed by the government of the United States, whose agencies really furnished headquarters for their fiendish operations. Had these wards of the government been put under military control, these raids would never have been made, and Chief Joseph would never have tried his scheme of cutting his way through the country, had it not been for the Custer massacre.

Custer's battle was the last one of any note fought by the blanket Indians of the plains. This last bloody stand, where three hundred and sixty-one men offered up their lives on the altar of their country, marks the sunset of a dying race, whose existence will continue to fade year after year, until at last the memory only shall remain on canvas, and on the pages of history and song.

Custer still lives in the heart of the pioneer, who tells the tale of the martyrdom to listening children, and in the coming time, the name of this illustrious hero will take a place not far below those of Washington and Lincoln, and grow brighter and brighter until time shall be no more.

CHAPTER VI.

On the night of August 20 we camped on the banks
of the Big Horn River, just opposite old Fort Smith, about
two miles from the canyon. The grass was three feet high ;
berries of all kinds were in abundance, with wild plums, crabs
and chokecherries. We spent a part of the time prospecting, and found gold, but in very small quantities. It looked
as though it had been carried in the current for a long distance. As we had been without fresh meat for several days
and were feeling the need of it, I shouldered my rifle and
started down the river. The heavy undergrowth of cottonwood, berry bushes, rose bushes and red willow impeded
my progress. Many wild ducks sailed near, tempting me to
shoot, but I was loaded for larger game and could not afford to waste ammunition. When about two miles from
camp I heard footsteps and the snapping of dried sticks.
The sounds seemed to come from behind a clump of bushes,
and in an instant my rifle was pointing toward the spot. I
advanced cautiously, made a close investigation, but found
nothing. Greatly puzzled, I plunged on through thickets,
thorns and water. I must have meat. It was a groundhog
case ; fat bacon was below par. I had eaten so much of the

salty stuff that I felt that I could drink the river dry, and was determined not to return to camp without a deer, elk or bear; even a coyote (canis latrans) would have been preferable to any more of that "sow-belly." My clothes were almost torn off by thorns and briers; I was a long way from camp and tired. Worse than all else I had not seen any game, had not fired a single shot. My resolution was fast giving way.

At last, weary and dejected, I turned to retrace my steps, when the stillness of the evening was broken by a rifle shot. The ball came singing through the air, close to where I stood. I heard the rustling of boughs, the crackling of dead underwood. The next moment a large white-tail doe came bounding into sight, like a cannon ball, trying to break her neck by leaping through the bushes. Waiting until she came to an opening, I drew on her and fired. On she went, bounding higher than before. I shot again and stopped her wild flight. The ball took effect in her neck, breaking it. The first ball had passed through her lungs and eventually would have resulted in her death.

The shooting brought the man who had fired the first shot upon the scene.

"Well," said he, "I thought I gave her a dead shot. She was running straight from me, and I aimed at her neck. There it is."

I soon convinced him that a deer could not run a quarter of a mile with its neck broken. He laughed and said:

"I'll go snooks with you on the old lady."

"That is very generous on your part and I am willing, provided you help carry it to camp," I said.

We cut out the entrails, cut off the head, tied the feet together, hung the doe upon a pole and started for home. What a load it was! It swung to and fro, nearly jerking us to pieces. When we arrived at camp the boys were profuse in their congratulations. Just as we were laying down our precious burden, bang! went a firearm, and Thomas Randall fell dead at our feet. The only words he spoke were, "Oh! dear," and the blood came pouring from his temple. Charles Swerts had been sitting near by playing with an old Colt's revolver, which went off accidentally, killing poor Tom. When Swerts saw what he had done, he threw himself upon the ground and writhed in agony of spirit; he acted as one distracted. With tears and sobs he begged the boys to kill him. We gathered around poor Randall, tears flowing freely from every eye. Men who had not wept for years broke down, as they looked upon the body.

Randall had joined us at Deadwood, after he had gained the consent of his parents, who lived in Chicago. Wustun informed us that he was of one of the first families in that city. He was always kind and helpful, ready for any emergency and a true gentleman. We buried him in the cemetery at Fort Smith, making his coffin out of the best wagonbeds we had, finishing it as nicely as possible under the circumstances. A mound was raised over his grave and strewn with beautiful wild flowers. Not a few tears fell upon his grave; as we felt an affection for him that only mountain men, who have roughed it together, can feel for each other. The day after the burial, as we were pulling out, I saw Charles Swerts, with his effects, leaving by himself. Some of the boys had objected to his traveling with the train after that fatal shot.

The country around Rotten Grass is a paradise for game. A dozen of us, myself included, started hunting, half of our number on one side of the stream, and half on the other, each eager to fire the first shot. "Look sharp; here comes a buck! head him off." A dozen shots were

fired at him, still he wavered not. One shot had hit his
hind leg. When he passed me, I gave him two broadsides
and he came to grass.

Some one called out, "A bear!" To say that we all ran
to get the first shot would not be doing justice to our loco-
motion; we merely touched the ground in high places. The
bear was in a thicket, and we sent in a large dog after him.
As he was charging the dog out we fired a half-a-dozen
shots, some of the boys hitting him. We had not gone two
hundred yards when some one on our side of the stream
motioned us to a large patch of wild plum bushes. He had
seen a large grizzly (ursus horribilis) go in there, which
we soon had corraled. I was on the upper side. Some one
below said: "Close in and let the hounds loose."

I stood where I could command a good view, and hesi-
tated about closing in; but, as I had never killed a bear and
was very desirous for a good shot at one, I obeyed the command, jumping the thorny bushes. I looked before me and
saw the bear coming straight toward me. I turned and tried
to run, but jumping down hill and up hill are very different.
The thorns caught my clothes and held me. On came the
bear, looking backward toward the boys below, who had
started him. I gave him a chance to change his route, but he
came straight ahead. He did not see me, but I could see his
turned-up nose and powerful claws, and my hair, in its endeavor to stand upright, fairly raised my hat from my head.
With my rifle cocked, I waited for him to come closer, hoping to get a shot at the side of his head or the butt of his
ear. In desperation I raised my rifle, gave a slight whistle
to call his attention, and, as he raised his monstrous head,
I gave him a ball just above and between the eyes. To my
relief he fell backward, tearing up earth and bushes, covering the ground with his blood.

I rushed up to stick my knife into him, but found his skin was like an old rawhide, effectually resisting my knife. An old trapper who was with us, told me never to do such a thing again. I have many times since had cause to remember his words. I had made a lucky shot, and thought a bear was not so terrible after all. All hunters know, or learn in time, that it is not safe to meddle with a wounded bear; some have learned it to their sorrow. When we got back to camp we found that together we had killed three bears and seven deer.

We stayed here the next day and spent the time hunting and fishing, with splendid success. In the evening we had another old-fashioned concert. We had come here expecting to find a pass into the Big Horn mountains, but no pass was to be seen. Our guide had brought us into a country of which he knew no more than did the rest of us, and we were obliged to return to the Big Horn River to make Pryor's Pass. Once more we settled down in the camp where Randall was killed. We swam the river in search of a crossing-place, and were rewarded by finding a gravel-bed which ran down the river, covered with about four feet of water in the deepest places. While searching for this crossing I found a butcher knife and an old six-shooter, with one charge out of it. Others found different articles of clothing, covered with blood-stains.

We were convinced that there had been foul work here since our departure four days before. We set out to unearth the mystery. The ashes of our campfires still lay scattered about; we noticed fresh dirt had been thrown upon them. With our shovels we scraped the dirt and ashes away and beheld the body of a man. There is no doubt that he was murdered. In the pocket of his coat we found a small packet, marked with his name, Harry J. Morris, Vinton,

Iowa, and a few portraits.   Scattered around were rings taken from a bridle bit, and we immediately suspected a man
named Frank Roberts, who came to us when we were here
before for the loan of a cold chisel to cut the rings off his
bridle bit.   We gathered all of the murdered man's effects
and sent them to Fort Custer with the details of the murder,
which was probably committed for money.   Our being driv-
en to the Big Horn was the means of bringing a guilty man
to justice, for sometime afterward the murderer was hanged
in Virginia City.

Rolling along toward Pryor's Pass, the mountains were
seen in all their grandeur.   The loftiness of mountains, more
than any other feature, fills us with admiration and awe, for
the same reason that the human soul, raised above the dross
of this world, calls forth our deepest love.   We were winding our way slowly around the base of the Big Horn range.
The Rockies in the distance towered upward until snow and
sky seemed mingling together.   We pressed forward in our
saddles, peering on every side that nothing might escape
our notice.   A great stretch of prairie lay before us.   Off
to the right some dark specks were seen.   They looked like
birds.   As we drew nearer, I dismounted and with my field-
glasses soon made out that they were really live buffaloes.
This was my first glimpse of these masters of the plains,
and a long one it was.   Then the desire to pursue them took
full possession of me.   Filling the magazine of my Winchester and inserting one in the breech, I communicated my
discovery to two of the men, who were riding fresh horses,
and they agreed to ride up behind the buffaloes and drive
them toward the train.

When the boys were partially beyond them, the buffaloes detected the scent, threw up their monstrous heads
with a shake, and, with tails standing straight up, came

thundering directly toward us. The boys followed as fast as their horses could carry them, but were left far behind. Having started out to meet them, I tied my horse to a wagon, and stationed myself near the mouth of a deep ravine; the others thought to meet them as they crossed the ravine. Instead of crossing, the buffaloes ran toward its mouth (where I stood) tearing up the earth with their great hoofs, their tails erect and their large, fiery eyes gleaming, looking like creatures designed to scatter death and destruction. As one came within fifty paces of me, he received a broadside, then another and another, until I had planted five bullets in his shaggy coat, when down he came with a thud that almost shook the earth. In a moment I was at his side, watching the black blood gush from four wounds and spurting from his mouth and nostrils. He did not relinquish life without a struggle, but continued to kick, tearing great holes in the earth wherever his hoofs came in contact with it, until the last breath had left his body.

"Now for a robe!" I said, and commenced to skin him with a dull knife; but, finding that his skin was three-fourths of an inch thick and that it would take two days to finish the job, I took the tongue and a large piece of the hump, leaving the remainder of my first buffalo where he had fallen. The boys killed another, firing fully one hundred shots at him before he fell. They were not in a position to get a good shot.

We continued our broken journey and soon found ourselves at Pryor's Pass. This swiftly flowing stream rises in the Pryor mountains, and is celebrated for its fine, large trout. A trip into the mountains convinced us that we were in the natural home of wild beasts. Going up the stream, we heard a rifle shot and found that Tom Houston had killed a silver-tip bear, about half grown. These bears make a savage fight when wounded.   They ransack the country, eating all kinds of berries, bugs and worms.   They are wonderfully clever in finding game that has been killed and left by hunters; I have known them to scent a dead elk several miles off.   A wounded animal stands no chance of recovery near one of these bears, for it is hunted down and devoured.

That bears are slow on foot and very awkward is an idea prevalent among people who have never seen nor hunted them.   They imagine that a good spry fellow can dodge them very successfully.   Let me give a word of advice to those who are thinking of visiting the Rockies to play with the grizzly for the first time.   The mouse does not play with the cat, but vice versa; a man in the power of a bear has little or no chance of escape; the bear is as quick as a cat in proportion to his size; what more can be said of the man and the mouse?   To hunt bears one needs a 45-60 Winchester, or something as good, if it can be found, and a sharp bowieknife.   Armed thus, a man may tackle the grizzly with safety, providing he knows how and when to use his weapon.

After the hunter has sighted his game, he approaches it as closely as possible, keeping on the leeward side.   He takes his stand near a tree, or where he will have some means of escape should his first shot fail to do its work. When all is ready, if he is unobserved, he draws a bead on some small object to see how it is with his nerves; if all is right, he takes a good breath, gets his rifle in position and gives a shrill whistle.   When the grizzly deigns to raise himself gracefully upon his haunches to take a look at the hunter, a bead is drawn just between the eye and ear; or, if he be facing the hunter squarely, a ball is given him in the center of the throat.   If the shot is well directed, one is apt to say, "Well! I don't think it is much of a job to kill a bear." If the animal is only wounded, it is the part of wisdom to climb the tree before it is too late. Many have lost their lives by underrating the strength of a wounded bear. Heavy undergrowths of brush and bushes do not slacken the speed of a thousand-pound grizzly, though it may sadly inconvenience the hunter. I have seen them mash down bushes three inches in diameter while making a charge.

Pryor's Pass stretches away like a small valley, affording ample room for travelers. While rounding a bend we came upon a young buffalo calf and gave him a volley which finished him. The report of our guns started up a band of antelopes. They came directly toward us, intent upon passing through the canyon, which would bring them within fifty yards of the wagons. We kept still until a number of them had passed, knowing that the others would follow or die, then the firing began. Some of our men became so excited that they fired at random at the herd collectively. As the antelopes dashed past like a flash of lighting, six were killed and wounded out of a band which looked to be five thousand in number. We took only a few hams with us, for antelope (antelocapra Americana) is not the finest eating to be had in the mountains, and we were well supplied with better game.

Sage Creek rises in the Big Horn mountains and flows into Wind River. The water is pure and the grass around it is of excellent quality. Wind River flows through the canyon of the Big Horn, and, as it emerges from the canyon, it takes the name of Big Horn River. Stinking Water, a tributary of Wind River, was so named by the Crows from several large sulphur springs found there, which are destined to become a great health resort. At this point our guide was not only again entirely at sea, but he had been for some time. To escape the consequences, he made an excuse to go after provisions, with a family on their way to the Crow Agency, promising to be back in three days. I was convinced that he did not understand his business, that he did not know the topography of the country in which we were, and that he had misled us from the first.

I tried to persuade my friend Mitten to turn back with me and go to some settlement, where he could find employment. He received this proposition with disdain. No, indeed! He was to have a gold mine, a corner lot in the new Eldorado. I had asked him several times to give up the trip with the same result. This time I told him my oxen should go no further—he owned the wagon and bedding and I the team. He became indignant and declared that our guide would be back as he had promised, and that I would upset everything by acting so. Finally I told him that I would go on just to satisfy him, and if Lyons (the guide) ever came back, the oxen were his; for that in my opinion Lyons was a scoundrel and deserved hanging. He made a great show of indignation and repeated my words to Lyons, just before he started. Lyons came around with two six-shooters, ready for use, one in each boot, thinking to scare some of us. We crossed the Stinking Water, where we bade adieu to a few of our friends, whose destination was Bozeman, and then kept on toward Wind River.

The scenery was charming. In the west the Rockies were more clearly visible than they had been before; the Big Horn mountains to the east looked as if they might be sentinels, keeping guard over their more majestic neighbors. The Bad Lands, to the south, somewhat marred the picture. They presented a very uninviting appearance. Notwithstanding we were surrounded by so much beauty, our hearts were very sad and heavy. Truly, there was cause for this feeling. Our provisions were nearly exhausted. Our teams were almost dead with fatigue and looking miserably poor. Before us were the Bad Lands, the worst in America, and these we must cross. We were upheld by the hope that, in spite of our doubts, we might find the glittering gold that would prospect thirty cents to the pan, and pay us liberally for our labor and hardships.

We went in the direction of Rattlesnake Range and passed the Owl Creek mountains; it was next to impossible to cross the Bad Lands. There are different stories told of the origin of these lands. Some think they have been subject to volcanic eruptions, and some have other theories wherewith to account for their present condition. The lands looked to me as though they once might have been covered with a great forest of trees and that this forest had been burned down, smoldering deeply into the earth. When you look at the rocks you must believe in the eruption theory, for most of them stand on edge, and have the appearance of having been hurled hither and thither. Our animals sank almost to their knees in this treacherous ashbed. Save here and there a few wild flowers of rare beauty, there is no vegetation.

CHAPTER VII.

A Strange Battle and Indian Horse Races—A bald eagle and a rattlesnake in a death battle—horse racing—Indian ponies successful—white men's strategy—large bet—Indians lose heavily—Indian riders.

On a beautiful September morning, as I was cantering along a mountain divide, drinking in the fresh air and admiring the beauty of mountain, river and forest spread out below me, the stillness was suddenly broken by the shrill scream of an eagle. High in the heavens I saw him, preparing to descend. Down, down, he came, with the swiftness of a shooting star, until he had nearly reached the earth, when he spread his powerful pinions, slackened his speed, and with a sudden swoop, alighted on a great prairie rattler (crotalus horridus), about five feet long. A battle, such as I had never before witnessed, began.

I rode slowly toward the combatants, getting as near as I could without disturbing them, and eagerly watched the progress of the fight. The bird was one of the largest of bald eagles (haliaetus leucocephalus) and the snake was a monster of its kind, fully three inches in diameter. The eagle, with its crest thrown backward, ran up to the snake and, with his wings, gave it a blow over the head which completely stunned it, just as it was in the act of striking at him with all its force. Quick as thought the eagle then caught the snake in his talons, soared about ten feet in air, gave it a furious shaking and let it fall to earth, where it lay coiled in a warlike attitude, rattling and hissing.

EAGLE KILLING A RATTLESNAKE.

The eagle made a second attack in the same manner, but the snake watched its chance, and, when the eagle was close enough, thrust its head between the bird's head and wing, and, with a desperate effort, wound itself around the eagle's body. It looked for a moment as though the powerful bird must die. But, with a violent flap of his wings, he broke the deadly embrace, caught the snake, gave it a number of jerks, and threw it down again. The blood was oozing from several places in the rattler's body and this seemed to make the eagle more excited than ever.

The antagonists now remained some feet apart and seemed to be resting, though the rattler kept up a deep buzzing, perhaps to intimidate the bird.

The eagle next tried another plan, wheeling around his enemy in a circle, but the serpent was acquainted with this trick and managed always to face him. Thus foiled, the eagle began to whip the rattler with the tips of his wings, his head well thrown back, but the snake dodged the blows. The eagle then made a feint, jumped to one side and struck the snake a fearful blow; caught it up by the middle and shook it until the snake was about to twine itself around his body, when he again threw it to the ground. Both then showed signs of great fatigue, but neither seemed inclined to give way.

The eagle ran round and round his victim, in every conceivable way, but still the snake managed to hold him off, until he threw back his head and made a desperate drive. The snake then struck with all of its force as the wing of the eagle came in contact with its head, and, while trying to again coil around the eagle's body, was caught and carried into the air, where it was almost jerked in twain. When it reached the ground its entrails were hanging out, and it writhed and twisted in great pain. The proud bird stood looking on with the victorious air of a pugilist who has won a world-renowned battle.

For the first time he cast his large eyes upon me, showing neither surprise nor anger at my presence. He seemed to understand that I would not molest him, for he turned to the snake and gave it another good shaking, to make sure of its death. I was tempted to take him home as a trophy of the battle, but his unshaken confidence in me unnerved my arm. When the agonies of death were over and his enemy had ceased writhing, he stretched his wings, seized his prey where the skin was not broken, and, with a steady flight, bore it to the highest crag of the neighboring mountain. As he slowly winged his way, the huge serpent was visible hanging from his powerful claws. The fight had lasted about three-quarters of an hour, and, had the eagle been less careful of his head, he could have torn the snake to atoms in a moment, but he seemed to realize the poisonous nature of the snake, and gained his victory by the exercise of his strategic instinct.

In the fall of 1877, the few straggling settlers and the Indians of the Yellowstone valley were seized with a mania for horse racing. Betting ran high, and, as the Indians were generally the winners, the boys were in very hard circumstances, owing to this strange passion, which seemed to have taken full possession of them. The best horse in the settlement had come out far behind a homely, little scrub belonging to the Crow tribe, and the boys were in despair until a bright thought struck them.

While the Indians were out gathering their winter supplies, the boys around Stillwater sent to Oregon and made arrangements whereby three renowned racehorses should be brought to them. They kept the affair very secret, for fear the Indians would hear of it. Early in September the warriors returned, with an immense upply of venison, dried buffalo meat and robes. They went into camp near the mouth of the Stillwater, and soon commenced bantering the whites to make races. Finally the boys agreed to race in two weeks. Every day they pretended to be training a large bay colt, which could not run at all, by galloping him up and down the track, in sight of the Indian camp. This colt was not to run, but the racer was another horse, which very nearly resembled him in color. This was a cunning device to deceive the crafty Indians and to induce them to make large bets. The race was to take place at dusk, some distance from camp, and the deception would probably not be noticed until afterward.

I learned the time set for the racing, and was glad that the down coach would land me at H. Countryman's in time to witness the event. The time was changed to three o'clock in the afternoon, and the settlers from one hundred miles around were there, all eager and excited. There were about four hundred Indians present, including squaws and papooses. The Indian racehorse was brought out, and the boys produced the clumsy bay they had been training. The Crows gather around him, looked him all over, commenced betting freely, but when the stake had reached fifty dollars, the boys refused to go any higher.

The race was to be six hundred yards. The horses were to start at the drop of a hat. The Indian rider was a boy ten years old, and the white jockey was a full-grown man. The white man got about six feet the start and kept whipping his horse with his hat, which scared the Indian pony from the track, but the boy gave his pony the raw-hide on the side of his neck, succeeded in getting him back, and, in spite of this loss of time, he beat the bay two lengths. Thereupon the air was filled with yells and howls, the squaws and papooses dancing in their excitement.

The boys pretended to be very angry, but said they had another horse which could beat him, so it was brought out, and this time the bets ran up to one hundred dollars. A little buckskin pony was selected this time by the Crows, and the boys gave the little fellows three cheers, which the Indians seemed to take as a compliment. The Indian pony got about three feet the start of the other and came out twenty feet ahead. This set the first race completely in the shade, and the whoops and yells could scarcely be endured. The Crows loudly ridiculed the boys, calling them squaws, and acted like men intoxicated. They said their hearts were good, their medicine was strong and they had a pony at camp that could outrun anything the pale faces owned.

The boys pretended to be very much cast down by this second defeat, which gave the Indians great confidence in their ponies, so finally the Crows brought out their champion race-pony, and offered to bet two to one that he could beat any horse the settlers might bring forward. The time had come for the boys to show their hand, so they led out Oregon Snail, covered with dirt, his head down, his mane full of burrs, and he really looked like an old cow.

The Indians laughed and hallooed, calling him a squaw pony, and made many other disparaging remarks. The Crows then bet forty head of ponies, all the robes in camp, and the squaws bet their moccasins and their entire stock of clothing, just received from the agency. The boys continued betting until sure that the Crows had staked everything they had, money included. The owner of Snail had a band of cattle, worth five thousand dollars, and he had also pledged his word to make good every loss which the settlers might sustain through extravagant betting.

The Indian racer, rode by a son of Birdshirt, was champing his bit and prancing around like a wild horse, but his rider was an expert and handled him well. Snail stood with head down, switching the flies with his tail until the word to make ready was given, when his rider, clad in a tight-fitting suit of silk, stepped forth, with a few light brushes cleared away the burrs and dirt, showing his glossy, bay coat, his heavy jet-black mane and tail, altogether a noble looking animal. His bridle and blanket were quickly adjusted, and, with his large eyes shining like diamonds, he evidently understood what was expected of him.

All was excitement among the Indians and whites alike. When the order was given Snail made a plunge in the air, with head and tail erect, and the Indians began to wonder what he would do. The Indian rider would not turn his horse square around, and kept him sidewise, first on one side then on the other, but was obliged to give up this trick. Both ponies were good runners, but Snail's first leap measured twenty-two feet. He kept ahead all the way around and came out forty yards in advance.

The Indians stood rooted to the spot as if stunned, while the boys raised a yell that cannot be described. Some of the vanquished cried, while others laughed, saying: "Pony heap good." The boys were more than recompensed, for the cash value of the bets amounted to from twelve to fifteen hundred dollars. Some of the squaws were barefooted, and the boys took pity on them and gave them back their moccasins. The Indians were so thoroughly outwitted they could not bear to remain in that part of the country, but as quickly as possible withdrew to the agency.

Indians are very good judges of horses and seldom lose a race. Their riders are always well-trained boys of light weight, but this event for a long time put a stop to racing in that section of the country.

3

CHAPTER VIII.

The country around Pryor Creek was, in early days, a
favorite resort of the Indian tribes of that region. There
was an abundance of game, consequently many skins were
to be had. Here many victories were celebrated by the joyful wardance, which was the outcome of many fierce, desperate battles. All the way from the mouth of the canyon
to the mountains, the scenes of past conflicts are pictured
upon the stone walls and upon every available rock, in true
Indian style. Warriors of the Crow tribe who still linger
around the spot, fraught with so many pleasing recollections, love to interpret the pictures and figures cut in the
rocks and wax eloquent over the recital of the events they
represent. Often in their excitement, in order to express
the intense hatred which they retain for enemies long since
passed away, they fire volleys against the rocks, where their
adversaries were wont to ride to and fro in battle array.

These pictures upon the rocks are to them what the
written history of our country is to us. And even a small
pile of stones may be the symbol of a great epoch in the
history of their nation. Rocks and stones are sometimes
placed in such a manner as to describe the position of the

contending forces.   A tall, straight rock, standing by one
lying down, represents the victorious warrior standing over
his fallen foe.   These symbols are placed in every conceivable shape and position, and represent many different events.

In the year 1834, it is said, the great Crow chief, Rotten
Belly, with a large number of braves, was camping near the
Big Horn River, when the news reached him that a Sioux
chief, famous in battle, was upon the warpath with a great
force under his command, and might bear down upon the
camp at any moment.   Rotten Belly in great alarm hastily
removed to Pryor Creek, and prepared for the fall hunt.
He thought his enemies would not molest him there, and if
they did, the nature of the country, when once they were in
it, would give his people some advantages over an invading
force.   Not many days after they had left the Big Horn, the
Sioux in passing discovered the ashes of their campfires,
and exulted in the prospect of a battle in the near future.

The sagacious Sioux chief, in order to ascertain something about the number of the Crows, placed ten of his warriors around each of the campfires, that being the number
usually allotted to a fire, and then proceeded to count them
in his own way, whatever that may have been.   There was
great rejoicing when he found that the Crows numbered
about three thousand, which was a small number compared
with his own followers.

The calm beauty of the night was sadly marred by
these painted, repulsive creatures as they went through the
motions of the wardance, burning sweet willows, and
"making medicine" until the horizon gave the signs of approaching day.   They were anticipating the easy victory of
which they now felt so sure.   Daylight found them upon the
road; for a hard day's ride lay before them, over a country
destitute of water, while the intense heat of the sun scorched

their bodies and increased their thirst. But these trifles disturbed not the tranquility of their feelings. They did not for a moment lose sight of the scalps and plunder that were sure to be their reward when all was over. So on they went, passing over the natural obstructions of the region with unabated courage, until they came within sight of the Crow encampment.

It would be difficult for one who has never experienced the fears engendered by the dangers of war, to imagine the consternation which seized the Crows when they saw their home hills, which encircled the place of their birth, covered with their most deadly foes. The sun, just sinking out of sight, made the prospect more dark, the scenes more wild and fearful. The impatient warhorses, decked with feathers, played well their part. The tramping of their hoofs as they beat the earth and the grass into fine dust, fell like a knell upon the ears of the Crows, who were unprepared for battle. They realized that they were outnumbered, twelve to one; their squaws, papooses, and, dearest of all, their ponies, were threatened with speedy destruction. Rotten Belly, mounted upon his horse, his war bonnet fully six feet in length, braided full of eagle feathers floating through the air, came riding forth, commanding his warriors to strip and mount their horses with all possible speed for the conflict that must soon ensue.

No sooner had the Crows filed out in order than the Sioux made a desperate charge. The thunder of horses' feet and the wild yells and circling columns produced an effect both weird and awful. The Crows were speedily overpowered and forced back into a mountain gorge, and Rotten Belly, realizing that unless something were done at once, his tribe would soon be massacred, resolved to resort to stratagem. He ordered his braves to follow him, and

GAUL, A SIOUX CHIEF.

Prominent at Custer's Death.

when they had reached a little rise on the hillside, he called to them in a voice of desperation, loud enough to be heard by the Sioux chief—who at first thought he was calling for quarter and halted his men—that the Great Spirit would come to their aid mounted upon a white horse, that strength would be given them to kill their enemies. And lo! at that very moment, there appeared at his side a large, white horse, bearing a white rider with yellow eyes. When the Sioux, who had heard the words of Rotten Belly, saw his prophecy fulfilled, they were panic-stricken, and, but for the commands of their chief, would have fled from the field.

The Crows, feeling confident that the Great Spirit was fighting for them, with an unearthly yell bore down upon the enemy. They pulled the warriors from their horses. They drove spears through them or crushed them to the earth with battle axes. The Sioux seemed rooted to the spot, stunned by the sudden turn of affairs. The Crows pressed forward to the work of destruction, singing their scalping songs, their chief riding in the van and chanting the bloody song with savage glee, occasionally stopping long enough to cheer on his braves in the name of the White Spirit.

Unable longer to bear the terrible slaughter, the Sioux turned and fled, but were pursued, dragged from their horses, scalped and their mutilated bodies tramped under foot. Thus were they slaughtered until the kindly darkness hid the few survivors from sight. Their squaws were taken prisoners, and the Crows claim that some of them are still living in captivity. The Sioux tell the same story and believe it implicitly. Since that battle the Crows have been firm friends of the palefaces, through their love for the White Spirit with yellow eyes, and they call the white man their good medicine. I heard this story from several different members of the Crow tribe and they all told it alike, varying only in minor details. What really took place can only be imagined.

In the fall of 1864, the story runs, Long Hair, a celebrated chief of the Crows, was camped on the Yellowstone and Alkali Creek and the tribe filled about eight hundred lodges. All were fully equipped for the fall hunt, but, when the time to set out arrived, several were taken sick. Each day added one or more warriors to the invalid list, and it became evident they would have to postpone the hunt to care for the sick and dying. The disease from which they were suffering was none other than small-pox. Long Hair and the medicine men retired to the main medicine lodge and exerted all of their skill to stop the plague, but the burning of roots, herbs and their strongest medicine was of no avail. In despair they were all helpless, while the warriors fell off like dead leaves from the forest trees. They burned their robes and blankets, reserving only the best red ones, which they presented to the sun to appease the wrath of the Great Spirit. But the disease still continued to spread, carrying off warriors, squaws and papooses, while their neglected ponies wandered away and were lost.

Finally all but forty of the lodges were entirely empty, and the plague subsided. Two young braves, unable to endure the loss of all their kindred, dressed themselves in their best costumes and told the few survivors that their hearts were bad, and that they were going to join their people in the happy hunting ground. So saying, they mounted their ponies and rode to the top of the hill. Before them lay a shelf of solid sandrock about one hundred feet above the waters of the Yellowstone, extending twenty feet over the ledge, while beneath the angry waters thundered through masses of broken rocks. When the two young braves reached the top of the hill, they dismounted, blind-folded their ponies, called upon the few who had followed them to meet them where the bad spirit would never more kill their warriors, leaped upon the ponies and started at full speed toward the shelf of rock. On they went; the brink was reached; with the speed of a deer, their ponies dashed into space, down! down! down! The savage howls of the warriors and a loud thud in the waters below, alone proclaimed the fate of the misguided braves. A large pile of stones marks the spot where the fearful plunge that sent two souls into eternity was made.

Carved on a rock close by is the image of the bird after which their tribe was named. Several small punctures in the rock, and leading directly to its heart, signify that the disease of which they died went straight to their hearts. On the same rock are the figures of several warriors in a leaning attitude, representing their feelings when first taken sick, while others are lying on their backs in their last sleep.

CHAPTER IX.

How a Mountain Lion met his Fate—First a bobcat, then an elk, then the terror of the plains.

One lovely fall morning when the leaves were yellow on the cottonwood, the wild plums were brown, the red leaves of the chokecherry bushes were falling, and bunches of berries hung in great abundance, I started from camp on horseback in search of adventure. The willow grouse and pheasants were harvesting the delicious fruit, and as we crossed the narrow valley they flew before us and settled in the trees. From some points of view these would have been enticing, but I was after larger game. My path lay diagonally across the foothills of the region known as Rotten Grass, a tributary of the Big Horn mountains, south of Big Horn canyon.

While ascending the foothills I noticed signs of bears and of mountain lions. This rough region is well adapted to the welfare of lions, which lie in wait for the game as it comes to water. Along narrow trails, with very steep ascents among the rocks, I led my pony. Large boulders were loosened by the hoofs of my horse and rolled down into the green pines below. Our path led to a beautiful park in the mountain terrace where the odor of bear was quite strong. Billy, my pony, tried to locate the danger and kept snorting all the while. Many holes had been dug into the ground, and logs had been turned over and

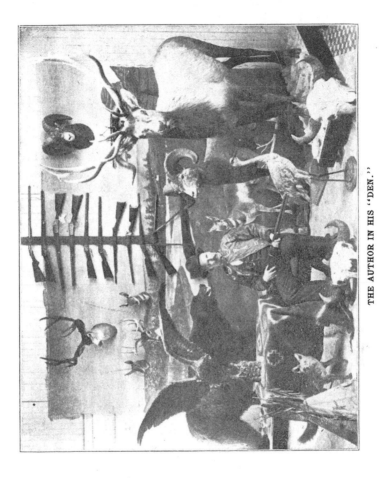

THE AUTHOR IN HIS "DEN."

the bark torn from the trees. Small bushes had been demol-
ished by bull elks brushing the velvet from their antlers.

The northern country was rough and broken, but I
located several quaking-asp thickets, and, knowing that
springs must abound there, I started toward them. Having crossed the park, I found many trails. I selected the
one most traveled and soon came to the remains of a bison
calf, killed the day before and partially eaten. I dismounted
for a close examination and found by fresh footprints that
a mountain lion, a bear, a lynx and some smaller animals
had been in the vicinity, so I made my way carefully down
the stream.

Presently I saw the sun glinting on the silken skin of
a bobcat which lay asleep. His paws were stretched out and
he was resting as quietly in the warm sun as though the
avenger were not on his trail. I quietly drew my rifle from
the sling, inserted a 45-85 cartridge and placed it on a line
with Mr. Bobcat's shoulders. I touched the trigger and
there was a sharp report. My victim gave one gasp, his
muscles twitched and with the jerking of his legs all was
over. His spotted skin has been reanimated by the taxider-
mist, and now adorns my den, where he watches a large
sandhill crane, forever silent, yet alert.

I now made my way down the ravine up which I had
come. There was a well-beaten trail leading directly
through this, and I was passing along at a rapid pace when
I flushed a band of twenty-five elks. They went off like
a flash, having winded me. I sprang from my horse in time
to see a calf just as it went quartering down the hill. My
first shot, which struck him in the flank, laid him in the
trail. I was soon on the ground, and found him to be a fat
fellow, though late and of course small. After his carcass
was secured behind my saddle I followed the band down

the canyon. Soon I found that an enormous mountain lion (felis concolor: known also as catamount, cougar, panther and puma) had been pursuing and that when I had flushed them, they all went the same direction. When I had gone about two miles I discovered that the lion had abandoned the trail and gone north.

Half a mile farther on I left the trail and took a mountain sheep path over a ledge of rocks. Here I found a bunch of five black-tail deer (cervus Columbianus) and could have killed them all, but they soon fled to the north. I followed in this direction, as it was campward, and was soon confronted by fallen timber and ledges of rock which were almost impassable. I walked, leading Billy, and finally came out on another trail which led in the direction of Rotten Grass, following the deer and the lion. The lion was a monster, evidently now on a still hunt after the deer. I believe he had been in my vicinity the greater part of the day, and I now determined to hunt him.

Coming to the creek bottom, I picketed my pony and let him feed while I took a survey. On rounding a large clump of bushes I found the deer had scattered and had come out separately. The lion had not yet come out. I was quite excited as I stood in a beaten trail just across a little creek. It seemed to me that I detected either a struggle or some faint sound. When I stepped forward to listen, all was silent, save the murmuring of the stream and the falling of the leaves. Some power held me to the spot, for there I stood, apparently without a motive.

At times I could hear a noise as if something were being dragged along, and suddenly I faced the trail across the creek, and saw the largest lion I had ever beheld, coming straight toward me. A black-tail doe was in his mouth, his head was as high as his long neck would allow, and the legs and head of the deer were dragging in the bushes. On he came, unconscious of my presence. As his eyes were elevated, I could hear him growl as if to satisfy himself, then lash his great tail from side to side, apparently feeling with it his way along through the bushes. His massive jaws were spread to their full extent, and he had crushed the deer's body until it was almost cut in two.

He advanced deliberately until he reached the gravel bar near the creek. I could see that he had torn a great patch of flesh just over the doe's heart, and as he deposited his treasure on the bar, a fiendish gleam was in his eye. He looked up and down the creek to see that the coast was clear, and then with his great paw, he turned the doe over as a cat would turn a mouse. He began to suck the blood that was oozing out of the great hole near the heart.

I stood motionless, hoping that some other lion would come and contest his right to this dainty morsel. Evidently he was uneasy, for as he walked round the doe, he would occasionally emit a low, deep growl, as if challenging all others to stand back. Meantime his long, snaky tail swayed continually from one side to the other. Something surely warned him of an enemy as he wheeled about and faced me. His bloody jaws were not more than forty yards away from me as he opened his mouth and showed a set of teeth dangerous in the extreme. He gave vent to a half howl and half growl which made the cold chills creep over me, although my friend, who never has failed, was between us.

Death had stared me in the face many times before, in many different forms, and the old Bullard had never been found wanting. In this trying moment my thoughts ran vividly over two bear fights, in which it looked as though the Supreme Being had interfered. I looked steadily into his eyes, but he did not cower. The bristles were raising

along his back and he looked like a demon incarnate. I
realized that in a few bounds he could be upon me. All this
ran through my mind as I slowly raised my life preserver
to my face.

I could see the platina ball through the rear sight, showing plainly on his throat just over the jugular vein. I was
calm now and gave the signal trigger a gentle pull. The
report sounded, and his grand attitude of daring, courage
and defiance was changed in the twinkling of an eye. I
sprang across the creek and saw him die. As I stood in the
lone forest, now again as still as death, save for this monarch in convulsions, I felt a pang of regret.

His great, muscular legs would stiffen as hard as steel,
and his long, sleek body expand like bellows till it was like
iron, then he would completely relax. His jaws would set
together like a vise, then open, disclosing his great ivory
teeth, which when once fastened in flesh, would never let
go. His motions gradually became slower until they ceased
and he was as limp as an eel. His arm measured fourteen
inches at the body, and he was certainly a perfect specimen
of his race. I have no doubt that hundreds of deer had fallen as his prey, but his day was now over. Soon his glossy
hide was strung to my saddle and I was wending my way to
camp. The doe was a young one and it was literally crushed
to pieces, the liver and lights having been torn out and eaten.

Presently I saw a band of twenty-seven deer, and could
have killed several, but let them take their way in peace. I
came out on the Rotten Grass Valley long after dark, and
saw our campfires far above. It was a welcome sight. I
fancied I could feel their warmth as the cry of the wolves
greeted me on all sides. My little Indian Billy soon got in,
and, after a hearty supper, my friends went with me over
the adventures of the exciting day and admired the skin of
the vanquished lion.

CHAPTER X.

We had landed on Middle Bowlder after two days' hard riding. Our packs were badly shaken up from a stampede that had been caused by an old she-bear and cubs. We were located about two miles below what we named "Devil's Slide," and our object was to get some saddles of venison and elk, for both deer and elks were there abundant.

It was autumn. The cottonwood trees were dismantled. The quaking asps loomed tall and white. A few leaves of gold and white still lingered. We were camped in the bend of the creek in a dense forest of cottonwoods, whose swaying branches kept up a continual warfare with the wind. The rushing water rippled over sands of gold, carrying pebbles of every hue. Here was the unmolested home of the mountain trout (salmo purpuratus), and, as I washed my dishes I could see hundreds of them of various sizes drifting idly through the sparkling waves. The mountain jays were chattering in the trees, and the magpies were alert for food—if it could be stolen at any point.

John Dunn, my comrade, had put away the ponies and was calling for water, for which I had been sent an hour before. While our weary horses satisfied their hunger in the great meadows, we made a supper of potatoes, salt pork and coffee.

"John, what will you breakfast on—elk, deer, mountain sheep, or trout?" I asked. "I have found that the creek is full of trout, and I saw fresh deer tracks in the park."

"Well, I am not hard to please, but if the sun will only wait an hour I will get my old sailor hook and we will have some trout. If you don't mind going up into the quaking-asp thicket, you may have a chance to get a white-tail, which would go nicely with trout."

I adjusted my belt, slung my rifle across my shoulder, and started up the creek. What a grand sunset! If old earth had been circled in flames, it could not have looked more beautiful. The western sky was almost scarlet. Floating clouds, passing over the snow-capped range, tinted with a thousand colors the canyons filled with cedars, and the bare mountain peaks which reared their heads until they seemed to penetrate the blue sky. The air grew calm and the waters seemed to hush their rippling. The elk stalked abroad, sending forth his challenge on the calm air.

My eyes fell on a band of red deer (cervus Virginianus) which had fed on the foliage fringing the creek, and, as I gazed on the faultless forms of the beautiful animals, I was stung with sorrow at the idea of killing such creatures. How long I stood there I do not know, but the shadows of the tall pines, which stood out like sentinels of the night, were casting long, fairy-like shadows far down the valley. The deer were now within a hundred paces, and would soon show me flags as they bounded over the red willows. I raised my rifle and slowly set the hammer at full cock. A fawn walked toward the lord of the herd, who seemed to caress it as he rested his great antler-crowned head against the fawn's shoulder, the while he gazed at me, his eyes sparkling. I changed my mind, and, as the sunlight sparkled along the barrel, I pressed the trigger, sending a bullet through the buck's heart. As if by magic a dozen flags went up, and, as the sun disappeared, I saw them vanish in the evergreens across the creek.

I went to the place where the buck lay, took his head and saddle to camp and prepared the head, which to-day adorns my home and often recalls memories of that golden sunset. In camp I found John frying trout for our supper. With broiled tenderloins, coffee, roasted potatoes, and trout, we feasted royally. In order to have him on hand early, I picketed my pony close at hand before we turned in, to be lulled to sleep by the rushing water of the creek.

Long before the break of day we were cooking breakfast, and, although the roasted potatoes were nearly all burned after passing a night under the cottonwood coals, we found sufficient, and before the light began to break in the eastern horizon, I was hurrying toward the mountain top. After several miles of climbing, I found myself in a little park, dotted with handsome cone-shaped pine trees, while the rimrock was covered with small cedars, junipers, and bunches of soap weeds.

While admiring the enchanting scene I heard a cry, long and pitiful, as though a lost child were near. It grew fainter and gradually died away, but was repeated at intervals. Day was breaking as the cry of the cat-owl was heard, coming from the far-off canyon; then came the cry from another direction. Could it be possible a child had been lost in this place? No, the plaintive cry is one never forgotten by the mountaineer or traveler who has heard it before. It was lonely enough on the mountain before day light came, but the dismal cries of the owls and cougars made it worse. Here and there I could see fresh tracks where some animal had been running, and, after I had tied my pony, I found hoof marks where mountain sheep had passed.

I was convinced that the cougars had been in reach of game, had separated, and were now calling to each other, so I went in pursuit of the first one. I passed through some timber, where it was dark as Egypt, my feet sinking deep in the soft vegetation and decayed pine cones. The awful silence was painful and seemed like a dream of the infernal regions. I pushed along a game trail, hoping to reach the upper rimrock. After going half-a-mile, I could observe I was nearing the ridge as light began to dawn. Jutting out into a pretty park was a splendid reef of gray sandstone about fifteen feet high, over which I could see the tops of pines in the park.

The songs of birds sounded on the morning air, and the little chipmunks and cottontails (lepus sylvaticus), also called Molly cottontail), skipped about, while the "camp-robbers," or mountain jays, were plucking the sweet pine-nuts from cones that hung low in great abundance. Some fool-hens were slowly sauntering along, scarcely leaving the trail as I passed. I had almost gained a break in the rimrock when I caught sight of a monster bighorn sheep (ovis or caprovis montana). He was not feeding, and seemed very uneasy. Soon I saw him bound up on a ledge of rocks, stand like a gladiator, whirl, and with head lowered, bound at something below.

My heart was steady, and I crept along as fast as the nature of the ground would permit. He had disappeared. No; for in a moment the bighorn reappeared on the scene, and stood gazing first above and then below him. I pressed the butt of the rifle to my shoulder and ran my eye along the barrel. Then I lowered it, certain that something of interest would soon transpire.

He stepped forward. His great brown eyes were riveted on some object on the rocks above him. Then he

dashed round a point by an old dead tree, and I thought I had been very foolish to let curiosity get the better of me. But I crept forward to a large rock and crouched under the boughs of an evergreen tree just as the bighorn rushed back and sprang to his old stand on the ledge.

I could see nothing but the bighorn. Was he crazy, or was he scenting danger? I was determined to find out what troubled him. I knew he could not scent me, for what little wind there was blew from him toward me. I stood up, defying the bighorn to run, well knowing I could cut him down with a shot. If he saw me he either dared not or would not run, and as I stood on tiptoe I caught the outlines of something above. Oh, those fiendish ears—that long, snake-like tail moving slowly to and fro!

I climbed upon the rock in time to see two monster cougars crouch low on the eareh. Closer to the ground they crouched, great cowards that they are, for they never fight an armed foe. They crouched still lower, till only their ears could be seen. The bighorn seemed paralyzed. He could not help seeing me, as I stood erect in plain view of him. I did not know what to do, but I crept up the rock in front of me and peered over the rim. The cougars had gone. The bighorn seemed to awake from a trance, and as he bounded away I fired. It was a weird, wild strain of music which the echoes awakened as the shot set the wild woods in a clatter from the magpies and jays.

The bighorn lay dying. The bullet had struck him on the shoulder and penetrated the neck. He was a beautiful specimen, with his great horns and autumn coat of blue hair. Could I have killed one of the cougars what a thrill of joy I should have felt. As I cut out a ham I determined to try for them next morning, believing they would come again, find the game, and feast upon it. Taking out the liver and heart and stripping the body of the skin, so that the cougars could not ruin the head, I departed by the trail over which I came, first having blazed several trees with my knife, that I might find my way if it should be dark.

Reaching my pony, I descended the mountain and found it was a great sheep country. I saw plenty of fresh signs, numerous trails had crossed mine since I ascended. I was leading my pony down the second rimrock when twelve large bull elks, appeared coming down the mountain, their antlers glistening in the sunlight like an army with drawn sabres. On they came with great strides, crashing through dead brush and over bushes, swinging their handsome heads with ponderous antlers lying well back, spreading the low branches of the pines.

They were entering a park when I fired at a large, dark-colored bull that was well in the lead. I had taken a quartering shot at him, but was amazed to think I had struck him in the back, for with the report his back jerked suddenly downward. All of the herd quickly disappeared. About four hundred paces down their trail I found my bull which had fallen dead without a struggle. On cleaning him I found the heart pierced a little below the center.

John was dressing a large white-tail buck when I reached camp. Night came on, and after a hearty supper we picketed the horses close to camp, and, seated near the glowing fire, related our adventures of the day.

"I saw your elks, Allen," John began; "they were going down the mountainside like a cyclone. They went down the creek and will cross about ten miles below here. They will run until they cross the running water; then they will stop."

"They are like Tam O'Shanter and the witches after the gray mare Meg," said I.

The night thickened into inky darkness, the wind howled, the trees were torn almost asunder, while the rushing water of the creek mingled its roar with the blast. But we slept through it all, to be awakened early by the alarmed chirping of some bird, as though it were at war with all its kind. After breakfast John said:

"I am going after those elks. What say you?"

"Well, John, I have a bait on the mountain, and will go there if you are willing."

Groping my way in the dark, I kept on until I had gained the beautiful park. I could hear game breaking through the underbrush, but could see nothing. I found the trail through the belt of green timber, and could see the blazes as they stood out ghost-like, seeming much larger than they really were.

Passing through the timber I turned in a opposite direction from that I had taken the previous day, found a break in the rimrock and made a circuit, keeping the old, dead pine as a guide. I had marked my ground well the day before, and knew just where to come upon my pets if they were at breakfast.

I examined the wind and found it blowing at right angles to my route. I took up a handful of dry grass and threw it as high as I could. The direction of any wind that may be stirring can readily be ascertained in this way.

Daylight had come. I rounded the tree with the dead top, and, with bridle reins over my arm, had gained a good footing on the soft rock. There was my sheep's head, the body, and even the horns, almost torn to shreds, and the great male cougar with his sides distended to their fullest extent, was standing over the carcass, snarling fiendishly at his mate.

She had backed up under a ledge, and was trying to

argue the case with her lord. His tail curled like a restless viper, lashing the air from side to side while he grew more restless. I stood there, but only a moment, and, as he tore a great chunk from the carcass, with his claws dug into it, I would have given anything I possessed for a picture of him with the sweet morsel in his great paws, and his fierce and threatening attitude. I sent a bullet through his skull. My horse sprang back and ran up the trail. The female bounded across the flat.

As the echoes of the first shot were thundering through the glens I gave her majesty a quartering shot, which struck her in the flank. She cried out, bit the spot as she ran, and rolled over. The second bullet caught her in the fore leg. Down she went, tumbling over and over. Quick as a flash I gave her a third shot, which stopped her. Scream and echo sounded and resounded, until the last wail of death faded away in the lowlands of the valley.

My horse had stopped and was feeding in the park, so I examined the battlefield. The male cougar's skull was completely crushed, his teeth knocked out, his brains scattered over the rocks. The 45-85-300 cartridge had been effective. After an hour's hard work, the skins, with my sheep horns, were in a portable condition. I killed a young bighorn sheep on my way back to camp.

Meanwhile three large golden eagles had almost ruined my elk meat. They were so loaded down they could scarcely fly. They had eaten out the eyes and then selected choice bits of the meat. One of them sailed over me so close I thought he meditated an attack on me, and as he circled round the second time I shot him. I secured his tail feathers, which are deemed very valuable among the Crow Indians, and hastened to camp as fast as my weight of trophies would permit. John had killed another white-tail deer. We hunted bears the next few days with satisfactory results.

BATTLE OF THE ELKS.

Reproduction of Russell's famous painting.

CHAPTER XI.

After a terrible pull we reached Wind River, our horses panting from over exertion. Here the grass was very poor, and, being obliged to find grazing for our teams, we went up the river about a mile, where we found a plentiful supply of good grass. At this place we were to wait the return of our famous guide. He had named the day and hour when he should rejoin us. After our late exertions we were greatly depressed in spirit. Something had to be done. We were out of meat and nearly out of everything else. As we were hundreds of miles from any settlement, in the heart of a great desert, and without any guide, many of the party gave themselves up to tears and bitter lamentations.

I was vexed for having been persuaded against my better judgment to travel into this desert, and took a wicked kind of pleasure in reminding the members of the company that, at a certain hour, our guide would appear like a good fairy and deliver us from our trouble. The boys were determined to wait for him, whatever might happen. Next morning I started up the river in search of game, which I knew could not be far off. I soon heard a bull elk (cervus Canadensis) breaking through the bushes with his horns and crept quietly toward him.   I saw his great horns, his black neck, his large gray body.   I stooped down, and, with my gun across my knee, aimed for his neck, which the shot broke.   As he fell back dead, three more elk ran out of the cover below him, and I succeeded in also killing one of them.   I could not bring them in myself and returned to camp to get help.   We dressed these elk, cut the flesh into slices, hung it upon a pole and dried it in the sun.   When properly dried, it is tender and delicious.

We had several days of waiting before us, so Nickelson, Mitten, and myself went off for a further hunt.   We were walking leisurely along when we espied above a sagebush a large pair of antlers.   We approached, Nickelson in advance, but he was in no hurry to shoot and kept edging nearer, peeping at the animal over the brush, when suddenly the elk scented us, and, with a bound, left us to ourselves.   We gave him a volley, but missed him entirely.   With my Winchester I had the advantage of the boys, who carried Sharp's rifles; when the elk was about one hundred yards off, I threw in a cartridge, and gave him a shot which took effect in his back.   This turned him at right angles, and I shot him through the lungs, but these wounds did not prevent him from taking to the woods at a good pace.

Just then smash, smash, went the bushes, as they gave way beneath his great weight, and we caught sight of him, struggling on, covered with blood.   Three shots rang out into the air, and he staggered, reeled like a drunken man, turned a short circle, and fell on his side at the water's edge. His violent struggles were bearing him out into the river, which was crimson with blood around him, when we dropped our guns and dragged him ashore.   Fourteen large and well-developed antlers graced his shaggy head, which weighed one hundred pounds.   This was a great prize to us in our present condition. We quartered him, hung him up and then started for camp by different routes.

I took the river bank, and, as I sauntered along, I noted numerous signs of game, and felt that it would not be a bad place to camp for the winter; but where were the provisions, the pack animals, the wolf poison, and other indispensables of a winter camp? Clearly such a camp would be impossible for us, and I dismissed the thought. Other signs I found were numerous, and the river banks were dotted with beaver houses. As I moved on, the signs of elk and bear became more fresh. The earth was entirely covered with hoof prints and the smell was unmistakable. I paused in surprise. Could it be a mule that I saw standing among the bushes? Impossible! There were no farmers in that country! On closer inspection I saw it was a large cow elk, with ears larger than a mule's and without horns.

Advancing a few steps, I saw there were fifty elk at least in view. I knelt upon one knee and took deliberate aim at my mule and fired. What a commotion it caused! What a rushing and thrashing of bushes! Bushes and small cottonwood trees were literally trampled into the earth. The valley and forest resounded with the clatter of hoofs. The boys renewed the firing from the other side and turned them toward the river. When the old bulls struck the water, the current seemed to stop. There arose a terrible din. The clashing of their horns against the trees as they made for the river, the noise of their hoofs and the splashing of water sounded like a hurricane in full blast.

I shot a large bull in the river, but he was trampled under the feet of his followers in the deep water and was seen no more; I fired at another one with giant antlers, just as he was plunging in. He was also hurled beneath the waters. We killed seven elk and recovered but one. There must have been five thousand of them. We could see them for miles, rushing up the rugged mountain, until they disappeared in a large, timbered canyon. We cut the horns off our elks and hung them in a tree.

I remembered that I had shot at a cow elk a little way up the river before the stampede and went back to look for her, but she had disappeared. I was almost sure that I had hit her, and could not account for her absence; I examined the ground carefully for traces of blood or hair, but none were to be seen. At last I observed a small tree, with a bullet mark upon it, where a ball had evidently struck it and glanced off; this explained the mystery. The tree had defrauded me of my cow. I was turning away when I caught sight of a fresh trail through the bushes that looked as if some heavy body had been dragged over it. I followed this trail, scanning every bush until I came to a hole in the ground, the size of a large hogshead, where the trail entered this slanting hole. Below I could see an elk calf. Further examinations proved that this was the den of a mountain lion. I cut a long and strong hooked pole, and commenced fishing for the calf. I soon heard a low rumbling noise in the cavern, and beheld, far down, a pair of glittering fire-balls. I drew a bead full between the eyes and fired. The flash and report of the gun, mingling with the dismal roar, was deafening, but quiet reigned within the cavern. My ball had sped home.

With my pole I worked long and hard and finally succeeded in pulling the calf above ground. I was very much surprised to find a bullet hole in its head. It was standing about thirty feet from the cow when I fired at her and the ball must have glanced from the tree and struck it in the head. This was the only way I could account for it. I wanted very much to see how it fared with my lion, but did not care to make further investigations. Assisted by the boys, we packed our game to camp and busied ourselves in drying it for future use. We were afterward very thankful that we had made this provision.

We had killed a deer the day before and left it hanging upon a tree. We thought it time to be looking after it, and went to the spot. Our deer was not here! The tracks of a large bear were visible, which explained matters, and, while the boys were gathering in the game, I took a turn after the thief. The deer was a large black-tail buck, and, as he was dragged along, he made a broad trail, which was easy to follow. It led me over brush and sandbeds for a long distance, but just as I was beginning to feel tired, I ran against my deer in a thick clump of willows. He was torn to pieces and covered over with earth and leaves, looking as though he had been placed there to remain. I waited patiently for a long time, expecting a visit from Bruin, but he did not make his appearance, so, after a thorough search of the surrounding thickets, I went to camp with the determination to visit the spot again before sunset, when he was sure to come back to feast off the deer. As the sun neared the horizon I cleaned my rifle, filled my cartridge-belt, put on a pair of Indian moccasins and started out alone. I always like to be alone when hunting bears, as there should be as little noise as possible. I approached, not a little anxious for my own safety. The grave-like mound had not been touched, and I knew that so far the coast was clear. After cutting a small opening through the bushes, I sat down by a cottonwood tree, with low spreading branches. A few of the thickest of these I cut off in case I should be forced to climb the tree.

I had been waiting what appeared to me a long time, when I heard a rustling behind me; I turned, and, not forty

yards off, was a monstrous cinnamon bear. He was standing erect upon his haunches, and seemed to be seven feet
tall. As I brought my gun into position, he turned and beat
a hasty retreat, but I gave him a shot from the rear. With
a roar like that of an infuriated bull, he charged upon me
so quickly that I could not get a shot, but dropped my gun
and took to the tree. He tore branches away and gnawed
at the tree in his rage. He then lay down to guard the tree,
lest I should escape his vengeance. At every move I made
he got up and renewed the attack. After a time either extreme thirst, or the pain of his wound, drove him forth in
search of water.

I climbed down with alacrity, picked up my gun and
started after him. He was wallowing in the water when I
whistled. He raised himself, received a ball from my rifle
and floundered out into deep water. I rushed in up to my
waist and caught hold of him, but too late, for I was fast
losing my footing and was obliged to draw back. My
prize had slipped out of my hands; I had nothing to show
for my perseverance, and the boys would not believe the
story if I told them, so I kept silent. On my way to camp
I killed a large wild cat—a poor substitute for my lost bear.

The time had now come for our guide to appear. The
last hour was gone. The sanguine ones, who were to have
rich mines and corner lots, began to droop. They found
themselves without money, with no means of getting any.
Lyons, with his smooth speech and ready promises, had
succeeded in relieving them of three or four hundred dollars. An indignation meeting was called, at which the fate
of the culprit was decided. Three men were to go after
him, bring him to our camp, and then he should be hanged
to the nearest tree. This was much easier to plan than to
do, considering our location and many other things. The

CINNAMON BEAR.

excitement was intense.   Many shed tears of vengeance, while others gave utterance to horrible oaths.

We could not stay here always.   It was time to move. Our teams were looking but very little better than when we stopped.   Our train numbered only ten wagons, the others having dropped off at different places.   After deciding to turn our faces northward and to recross the Bad Lands—but by another and a better route—we got our effects together and moved out.   Some held back, saying they were going to winter in the valley, but their real intentions leaked out later.   They were to remain a few days, while we went ahead and made roads, which they would follow at their ease—a cunning trick, but they did not get the better of us.   Ten miles or more brought us to a washout, which we could neither cross nor go around.   The only thing we could do was to make a bridge of driftwood and sagebrush.

After we had crossed, we burned the bridge behind us, to teach a lesson to our smart friends in the rear.   When they came to this place they were completely confounded. We had used up all of the loose material, which compelled them to camp there two days, and haul timber five miles with which to make another bridge.   They gained nothing by their selfishness.   But it was slow and hard work pulling through the Bad Lands, and we were very much pleased when we found ourselves once more on solid ground.

Off to the south, on a little knoll, we saw five buffalo bulls grazing.   Jack Woods and myself were well mounted upon half-breed horses, and we were soon skirting the foot-hills in hot pursuit.   As we came within seventy-five yards of them we lodged balls in two of them.   They thundered up the long stretch of tableland, we keeping as close as we could.   Our ponies would slacken their pace in spite of all we could do when they were close enough to scent the animals. I attempted to fire again, but the shell stuck fast, for in my haste I had snatched up an old needle-gun from one of the wagons.

On we went, plunging over stones and ruts. With renewed hope we saw the wounded ones lagging behind the others. All were now nearing the edge of the precipice, and we thought we had them cornered. Nearer and nearer they got to the edge, turning neither to the right nor to the left. The foremost one came to the jumping-off place, and with gleaming eyes and tail erect, made the fearful leap fifty feet below.

The others followed in the same manner, and all alighted in a sort of swamp, where they struggled violently, trying to make their way through the mire. Jack stood upon the edge of the precipice and gave them a volley while I was cutting the shell out of my gun. By this time three of them were out of the swamp; we fired at one of those left behind, and he stopped to battle, his head down and back arched, like a bucking mule.

"Give him one, Allen, to see him buck. I will try his hump," said Jack.

"I think I will tickle him a little," I said, and fired.

The buffalo reared and plunged, and rushed at his companions, as though he held them responsible for his condition. Jack shot again. The bull switched his tail and came toward us, mad with rage. A shot from my old cannon set him to waltzing in great shape. It was a first-class circus. We gave him thirteen shots through the body before he fell.

We amused ourselves in like manner with the others within range. Two escaped unhurt. Two were almost buried in the mire. The other one lay dead upon the ground. We secured the tongues of these three and went to camp, delighted with this little adventure.

Once more we found ourselves on the Crow reservation, near the Rosebud River, the waters of which are filled with mountain trout. The hills were clothed with bunch grass, whereon ponies and cattle were roaming by thousands, or basking in the mild Indian summer weather. The place was a picture of calm content. The grass swayed to and fro in the soft September wind. On every mound were the wily warriors of the tribe, gazing with satisfaction upon the scene, their red blankets lending an additional charm to the view as they strolled up and down, singing war chants, now and **then** stopping to dance to their own music.

Looking upon them in this peaceful attitude one could hardly believe them to be so cruelly savage by nature.

The smoke of our campfires was soon curling slowly upward into the mountain. The cattle had satisfied their hunger and were lying down to rest. A supper of dried elk and trout was soon prepared. It was then that the noble red men came over to smoke the pipe of peace with their pale-faced brothers, to eat of our venison and trout, and to drink our coffee. Our hospitality filled their hearts with peace, and made them feel that it was well to be at peace with the "masta scheely" (white man). We entertained three of them on this evening, and their faces fairly glowed with brotherly love as they looked upon the repast we spread before them. Our red friends distanced us in the race, however. We chewed our meat while they disposed of theirs in a way known only to themselves. When the last scrap had disappeared, they gave us a hearty hand-shake and departed.

At Deer Creek, on the Yellowstone, we stopped for a few days. It was surely Deer Creek, for we jumped three deer in camp before our teams were unhooked. I fired at a large white-tail buck on the run, and knocked off one of his horns. He went down, but he got up again and flew over the ground. Rifles were banging all around. Five deer rushed out together. I killed the leader and some one killed a doe. Our camp was in a whirl. The deer were bewildered, running in every direction. I followed the buck that I had first hit, and found him lying on a small island. He started to run, but I caught him in the neck with a ball.

Our teams having rested, we started again, and it was not long before we pulled into Bozeman—the most ragged, filthy and destitute lot of travelers that ever crossed the range. None of us had enough clothing to cover his body. I had a little money, but scarcely enough to buy a pair of overalls. With this I crept up a back alley to the clothing store of Ellis & Davis, and they let me have a pair. I found employment and at the end of two weeks bought a suit of clothes, after which I could walk the streets without a sense of shame. The other boys did likewise, and we felt quite proud of ourselves. Here we parted, with kindly feelings toward one another and went our separate ways.

CHAPTER XII.

I soon tired of life in Boseman, and found employment on the stageline running from Boseman to Miles City, a distance of three hundred and forty miles. We had no regular time for making trips, for it was impossible to foresee what might happen to detain us upon the road. At every station we would stop to get a fresh team, but often found that the horses had been stolen, the man in charge frightened away, or, worse still, that the station-house was in ashes. While making these trips, up and down, I became acquainted with a great many people along the route.

One of these was Hiram Steward, who had been leading a roving life in the mountains in search of gold and large game for twenty-five years. Steward was an old man then, six feet and two inches in height, well built, and as brave and fearless as a man could be. In one of his adventures he had been shot through the thigh, which shortened his leg and retarded his movements. He was stopping with Hoskins & McGirl, at Baker's battleground, on the Fort Custer crossing. This was the best stopping-place along the line, and was a favorite resort for the hundreds of hunters and trappers in the territory, owing to the genial qualities of the proprietors and the plentiful supply of well-cooked food always on hand. Hunting and trapping were lucrative employments. Meat, skins and furs found ready sale, and outfits were made up daily for a sojourn in different parts, in quest of game.

It was here I met Hiram Steward the second time, after I quit the stageline. I found the old man making up his packs, getting ready to start the next day. I was seized with the desire to accompany him, but, not wishing to push my company upon so famous a hunter, I managed by strategy to get an invitation. A hunter prizes a good, strong knife, so I went to work and made him one, with a blade eight inches long, and a long buckhorn handle, finely polished. The old fellow was delighted with it, and offered to go in partners with me on the hunt. It was a good offer, as he was furnishing meat for Hoskins & McGirl. I helped him, and the packs were all ready by noon.

After dinner, we gave our guns a good cleaning, and then went into the yard to shoot at a target. Steward never indulged in this sport, but liked to watch others. I was very lucky and beat the champion shot of the Crow tribe, which pleased the old man. He had looked at my Winchester with contempt, calling it an old popgun. His weapon was an old Sharp's rifle, of the first issue. For my trip I borrowed a buckskin buffalo pony, which had a great reputation as a runner. The evening was spent by most of the company in shuffling pasteboards, while I cornered a Crow and had him give me a lesson in his language.

Morning dawned. The sun rose bright and warm as on a summer day. We were soon upon the road, with four pack-mules, which we proposed to bring back laden with meat. We traveled down the river until we struck Razor Creek, which we followed into the Bull mountains. The antelopes seemed anxious to inspect our caravan and make our acquaintance, following us and stamping their feet all the while, as though they regarded us as intruders in their country, and were bent on having a settlement; but we were after buffaloes and did not heed them.

A march of two days brought us to the head of Razor Creek, where the Sioux had camped, to steal all the ponies they could find and appropriate the game, which was scarce in the vicinity. We made our camp in a secluded spot, among thick pines that kindly hid us from view. Early the next morning, after a hard tug, we reached the top of the range between the Yellowstone and Musselshell, and, with perspiration oozing from every pore, we gazed upon the country for miles around. Finally our eyes fell upon five large buffalo bulls, not far off. Sneaking up a snag in the hill, we came within three hundred yards of them and opened fire, when they made off like the wind and soon disappeared, leaving a cloud of dust behind. We hunted until we were too tired to hunt longer, and started empty-handed for camp.

Presently a large black-tail deer crossed a little bank, about fifty yards ahead of us. We started after him with all the speed we could make. When I reached the bank, I saw the buck and four others that he had just met, about to climb a hill. I fired and the shot made the hills resound. The buck turned with a bound and fell dead. An old doe turned to see what could be the matter, stopped, raised her head and stuck up her large ears, her black eyes shining like two great beads. The instant she paused, my Winchester spoke to her, and, as the smoke cleared away, I saw her lying on the ground, her neck broken just below the ear.

Steward stood like one petrified, making no motion to shoot. The other three went on climbing the hill. With rapid shots I brought two of them down, and, as the fifth neared the top, I shot him and he fell, but picked himself up again. I fired the second shot, knocking him down, but again he started to his feet. The third shot missed him. Five deer with seven shots, four killed and the fifth wounded. The firing was so rapid that one report had not died away before another followed, waking the echoes from hill after hill.

"Wal, that beats me!" said Steward; I thought you was a 'pilgrim' with a gun."

" A 'pilgrim' compared with yourself," I replied, "but I have used a gun before."

"Wal, then, why don't you get a Sharps?" said he.

"Simply because I prefer the Winchester."

"Have you ever been on the buffalo range?" he queried.

"No."

"Wal, I thought so; when you tackle them ar bar, you will larn more."

"You are right," I said; "but how do you like the Winchester for deer and small game?"

"Oh! it will do for boys to kill birds with, sure; but she don't carry enough lead for bulls and bars. If you'll just take a turn over the hill after that other chap, I'll get these ready to pack."

I started after the wounded buck and was crossing the hill when he broke cover from behind a log. As he was crossing the next hollow I gave him a ball in the shoulder and another in the back. He made a hard struggle for life but the lead was too much for him. His shoulders were terribly mangled, not worth saving, but the hams were good. On returning to Steward, who had finished his work, I found him admiring the knife I gave him. He had cut off the deer's legs to try its mettle, and found the temper sufficient to stand the test.

It took us about an hour to go to camp and get our pack mules, and, after we had secured the first four deer, we went for the fifth one and were surprised to find the shoulders torn to pieces and that the hams had disappeared. From all indication we concluded that a bear had paid him a visit. Tying the mules, we followed the trail up the canyon until it went under a large rock. The water had washed over this rock, making quite an excavation beneath. The bear evidently had found it a good hiding-place and had made it larger. Into this place she had taken herself with the hams of our deer.

Steward got a long pole and prepared for business. "When I punch her out, you take my gun and shoot her," he said.

"Thank you; if you are going to punch her out, I will take a seat on the top of this rock and try my Winchester on her," I said.

He made a thrust into the hole with the pole. The bear caught it and broke it into pieces. This made Steward very angry. He raved like a madman.

"I'll—I'll blow her out with a torpedo!" he yelled.

I wondered where the torpedo was to come from, and soon learned. He took a short piece of rope, pulled the twist out of it, filled it with gunpowder, and then twisted it up again. He then took a large handful of powder, put it into a small buckskin sack, and dropped the rope fuse in with it, leaving about ten inches hanging outside. He then wrapped the sack with twine until it was as hard as a cannon ball, tied it to the end of a pole, and set a match to the fuse.

"Now, look sharp," he exclaimed, "it'll make the old varmint vacate them premises and no mistake."

Forthwith he thrust the pole in as before. The bear

grabbed it with a snarl and broke it off, carrying the torpedo with her. A growl from her, an oath from Steward, commenced the circus. The torpedo burst, making the earth tremble. The bear and a thick volume of smoke simultaneously shot out of the earth, and Steward, who had not had time to get out of the way, was knocked down by the bear and rolled down hill with her. The bear, her hair scorched almost off, took no notice of Steward, but kept on, going up the opposite bank, and I thought I would never be able to shoot for laughter. Steward went one way, and his hat another. There he lay, looking as though he might have fallen from the clouds. I pulled myself together with an effort and sent a ball after the bear. She gave a roar, caught at her ham with her mouth, and came trembling and growling down the hill. I called to Steward that she was coming. It was a sight to see him recover himself and get out of the way. Bare-headed and with no gun, he came hopping up the bank. It was more than my gravity could resist. He grabbed my gun and rushed down to within thirty feet of her, and continued firing until the shells were all gone and her head was in pieces. Not satisfied with this, he took out his knife and disemboweled her on the spot.

"Now," he yelled triumphantly, "take the shoulders next time and leave the hams, if you don't want to git into trouble."

He was blind with rage, and swore he did not know whether the bear had ran against him, or whether the powder had blown him down hill.

"I believe I blew her clean out of the earth. I never saw her come out," he said.

"But what took you down hill so fast?" I asked.

"I give it up. She must have run agin me," was the old man's reply.

We left the bear where she was. She was poor, and her hide was burned through in places. When we had almost reached camp we saw something upon a rock.

"A sheep, by gracious!" said Stewart, and he bounced on ahead. He raised his gun, stuck out his foot, took a long aim and fired. His nerves must have been in a bad condition after his fright, for there was no movement upon the rock. He fired again, with the same result. I reinforced him and we fired together. Down came a large buck, shot clear through the chest. The ball was found in his backbone.

"Cuss that pea-slinger of yours!" said Steward, as we we were packing our game upon the mules.

"You will fall in love with that pea-slinger before we get through, mind what I tell you."

"Oh! ho! They are good for boys to larn with," grumbled the old man.

As we reached camp almost exhausted, the sun was hiding below the western mountains. Its departing rays fell upon the green hills dotted with pines, making a beautiful picture. Meadow larks were singing their evening songs, red squirrels were frisking and chattering in the pine-trees, a bald eagle soared with steady wing high over our camp, surveying both earth and sky. We gathered pine-knots and soon had a blazing fire, which sent clouds of smoke far above the pine-trees. Our supper was soon prepared and eaten, and, when the things were cleared away, Steward sat down, with a huge pipe between his teeth, sending forth clouds of smoke now and then, which almost darkened our camp. He was now perfectly happy, and could talk and laugh about unearthing the bear without a volley of oaths.

The next morning we made an early start for home, as Hoskins had requested us to be back as soon as possible, for he was almost out of meat. On the way we saw a deer standing not far off, looking at us as we moved slowly along. Steward dismounted and fired three shots at him, but the deer never moved. I began to think he was dead in his tracks, but a shot from my rifle brought him down with a bound, and we hastily lashed him to our pack animals. He was a mule-deer(cervus macrotis) and these are very stupid. We reached the ranch at four o'clock one afternoon, and promised ourselves that we would bring in buffaloes next time.

CHAPTER XIII.

Before a week had passed, Steward and I were on our way up Pryor Creek, to bring in another supply of meat. This was one of the best hunting districts in the West. The country was full of deer, elk and antelopes. We made our camp about ten miles up the stream, on a small tributary coming in from the West. There was a spring close by, and we had no fear of dying from thirst. Our camp was at the foot of a large cottonwood, with wide spreading branches reaching over all, making a very comfortable roof. The larks, like ourselves, were deeply attached to this tree, and made music in its branches all day long.

We turned the pack animals out to graze, and were making a fire, preparatory to cooking supper, when our attention was called to a band of elks quietly grazing up the stream, all unconscious of our presence. To the north, on top of a little hill, we saw a band of deer. The fawns were running about, playing together as frisky as lambs, the old ones alternately grazing and looking around them.

On an elevated spot below us, in a valley, was a large band of antelopes, that were considerably disturbed by our presence. Some of them were stamping their feet in a threatening manner, as though they fancied they could scare us from our bower. What a glorious opportunity for a hunter! The game was almost at our door and in large numbers. We felt like picking up our rifles and tackling them at once. But supper was to be cooked, and various other things done preparatory to the morrow's slaughter.

Next morning, before the sun was visible above the mountains, we were ready to grapple with any kind of game. The morning was very bright, but not brighter than our hopes for the day. The first game we espied was a band of thirty-two elks, lying in a cove between Steward and me. He had come out on a ridge and I had taken a route below him. I sneaked up to the mouth of the cove, as their faces were turned that way, and if startled they would be likely to run in my direction. When within seventy-five yards of them, I lay down behind a rock, and was just taking aim at a large cow that had risen, when the crack of a rifle startled me, and the cow fell to the ground.

By this time the others were upon their feet and making toward me in great fright. The foremost one was a calf, about one year old, and I killed it at the first shot. The next was a large bull. I threw in another shell and drew a bead for his heart. Though he was badly hit, he did not stop. I shot at a two-year-old cow, missed her, fired again, and brought her down. The band was now too far off for another shot. The wounded bull ran about half a mile and dropped.

Steward had forestalled me on the first cow, and killed another while they were running, which gave us five large fat elks, not a bad day's work. We packed them to camp, and next morning, after a hearty breakfast, made ready for the home trip, our mules having as much as they could carry. Steward took the meat home, promising to come back the next day, while I stayed to care for the camp.

ELKS, PHOTOGRAPHED FROM LIFE,

In the Gray Bull Country.

When I awakened next morning I could hardly shake off the feeling of loneliness which came over me.   After breakfast I walked over to the dividing ridge, to view the country and scare up some game.   I had walked about three miles when suddenly I came upon a band of antelopes, lying at the foot of a precipice.   Not wanting any antelope meat, I lay down and watched them.   They were feeding slowly toward me, enjoying the rank grass thoroughly.   All at once they scattered like a bevy of quails, and, looking up, I saw a mountain lion leap off a shelf rock, far above them, his long tail straight and rigid as steel, and his body extended to its full length.   He came like a bullet from a rifle, and alighted upon the back of a large antelope with such force as to almost crush it into the earth.   The shock killed it almost instantly.   The lion seized it fiercely by the throat, tore the flesh from the bones for about fifteen inches downward, and sucked its blood.   Then he walked around the body in a meditative manner, and began tearing the flesh from over the heart.   Having made a meal, which took about one-third of his prize, he seized the remainder in his mouth and came in my direction.

About fifty yards away he stopped, laid down his burden, raised his large, ugly head and looked toward me for fully two minutes.   Not desiring to share the sad fate of the antelope, I kept perfectly still, waiting to see what the lion would do next.   His lordship took another look at his prize, to see that all was right, looked furtively around and walked off.   My curiosity was satisfied, but not my sense of justice.   I wanted to see the savage beast laid as low as his victim.   I carefully raised myself to a sitting posture, got my rifle ready, and bleated like a young fawn.   He turned immediately, his whole attitude bespeaking suprise that any animal could have escaped his careful scrutiny.

I aimed for his hind legs, high up in the hips, and fired. The ball went straight and broke his legs, he gave a pitiful howl and tried to get up the hill, but found it was impossible. He then turned on me savagely, and would have annihilated me in no time could his broken legs have supported his heavy body. He cried like a good fellow, begging for the mercy that he had never shown to man or beast, but, after what I had just witnessed, I was not inclined to be merciful, and gave him a ball in the head which quieted him forever.

After walking another mile I found myself close to a band of elks feeding in a canyon. They were moving very slowly and seemed a lazy set. The bulls had shed their ponderous horns and there was nothing striking about their appearance. I was tired, and did not care to open upon them at once, so I lay down under a tree and watched them. Finally they came to a standstill upon a grassy hillside. It was too good a chance to be lost, and I roused myself sufficiently to cover a large bull with my rifle. The report startled the animals, but they could not determine from whence the shot came and knew not which way to run. This is a characteristic of elks and black-tail deer.

They almost always get bewildered when attacked, and often stand crossing their necks, turning and crowding together, until the hunter has time to kill all of them. When the smoke curled upward, I saw my elk dragging his hind legs upon the ground, but still he had the use of his fore-feet as I had hit him too high up to entirely disable him, although the ball had broken his spine. I paid no further heed to him just then, but continued shooting at the others until I had killed seven. I might have shot more very easily, but knew we could not care for a greater number at one time.

I now turned to the wounded bull. It had stumbled over a log and fallen into a little ravine, containing about three feet of snow. I walked up and took him by the new horns that were beginning to show. They were about four inches long and were still soft, and, as he made very little resistance, I stood in front of him on a small log and thrust my knife into his throat. While he was struggling to get out of my reach, the log I was standing upon rolled over and I fell beside him, almost under his feet. My feelings at that moment were not agreeable, for the blood spurted into my face and all over me, and he tried to stamp me with his forefeet. Had not his back been broken, no doubt he would have beaten me to death.

I cleaned and carved my elks, hung them upon trees, and went to camp hungry as a wolf, covered with blood. Steward was not there, as he had promised. The next day came and went, but he did not appear. I had a large load of the choicest cuts and did not dare to kill any more game, but, with only my gun for company, I wandered over the hills, watching the deer and elks feeding or basking in the sunshine. I was so lonely that my own shadow was a welcome sight.

On the fourth day after Steward's departure, I was favored with a visit from three Indians. I met them at a place where I had killed a young elk calf. They examined the calf, said it was very nice, and one of them asked if he might take it to his squaw, so I gave it to him. Immediately he squatted down, and broke its bones just below the knees with his meat axe, then forced the marrow out of them with a stick and swallowed it greedily, now and then taking time to grunt "itsic" (good.) Before leaving, they asked me where I was camping, and, without thinking of the probable consequences, I told them.

Steward came back about noon of the fifth day, and, while we were out packing our meat, these same rascals went to our camp and stole everything we had, excepting the tent. Upon our return to camp, we went for some biscuits and potatoes that had been left from breakfast. The red man's moccasins led the way, but no potatoes nor biscuits were there. With their little hatchets they had cut down five elk hams that were hanging to the limbs of our cottonwood. Perhaps they thought they were only taking their own, as we had killed plenty of game upon their reservation.

Steward looked around until he had taken in the extent of our losses. He then threw down his hat as though he were challenging some one to mortal combat, plucked at the few hairs upon his head, and swore by the red arms of the war-chief, that he would have revenge before anything else was done.

Night was approaching, and I felt that it would be both foolish and dangerous for us to tackle the reds at such an hour, so I tried to mollify the old man.

"Better wait until morning," I said, "then we will follow them up and have satisfaction out of them."

He went on like an unreasonable child, until his passion cooled down somewhat, when we made a supper of elk meat and rested comfortably upon our horse blankets.

When we reached the ranch the same day, we found that Crazy Head, a great chief among the Crows, and his band were stopping near. I spent the greater part of the next day lounging around the Indian camp, observing their actions, and gleaning some ideas as to their inner life from their talk. They were preparing for a long journey, therefore all the sick must be cured before the start. They went through the entire course of their medicine-making, and the

sweat lodge was full of patients most of the time. I saw
five braves strip and enter the lodge, which was made of
willow switches, stuck in the ground far enough apart to
form a small room, the tips of the switches being brought
over at the top and tied.

During the curing process the tent was entirely covered
with skins and blankets. A hole in the center of the room
held a number of small stones that were heated red hot, and
around these the naked patients ranged themselves; then
an old squaw named Two Belly, after making various kinds
of gestures toward the sun, poured a pailful of water upon
the stones. The room being very close, the steam arose in
such great volumes as to shake the slight structure.

The squaw then commenced warbling the medicine-song
song, the patients joining with a low, guttural "Hay a hay,
hay a," that was kept up as long as they could endure the
steam. At a signal given from the outside, the squaw threw
open the door, when the patients rushed out and leaped into
the river, where they splashed and kicked until tired out,
when they came to camp, wrapped themselves in blankets,
and lay down to sleep.

The squaw insisted upon my going in with the Indians;
"Heap good!" she said; but I told her that although it might
be good for an Indian, it was not for a white man, and that
I would rather peep in from the outside. They had great
faith in the sweating process, with much reverence for the
medicine-lodge and the medicine-man.

I had a long talk with Crazy Head, and he told me
about some of their customs and beliefs. When they are
going to fight an enemy, a warrior, mounted upon the finest
war-horse belonging to the tribe—horse and rider bedecked
with skins, beads and feathers, and painted in war-colors—is
sent through the village, to call the braves together. They

assemble at the council-lodge and decide upon the course to be pursued, while the medicine-men in the medicine-lodge are conciliating the Great Spirit in the following manner. Gathering all their most sacred articles, such as herbs and owls' feathers, they throw them upon a fire in the middle of the lodge. The chief medicine-man sits by, calmly smoking his pipe, and, raising it aloft at intervals, he importunes the Great Spirit to smoke with him. The burning process is continued until all the material is consumed, when the pipe is laid aside and all walk round and round, the medicine-men chanting a war-song, which is a prayer to the Great Spirit that his spirit may go with them in the battle, and turn away from their enemies.

I have often noticed that Indians are afraid of the dark, and that they seldom travel after nightfall. I asked Crazy Head the reason for this, and he said that they believe bad spirits are abroad in the night, and that the spirits of wicked Indians, long since dead, prowl around at night in the forms of beasts of prey. The breaking of a twig, the least noise at night, they attribute to evil spirits, and quake with fear at hearing them. They have a great dread of snakes, and cannot be induced to touch or kill one, as that act would poison their medicine, and they would never more have any luck when hunting.

When their health is good, and they are well supplied with game, their hearts are good, and the heart of the Great Spirit is good to them. When in this happy mood, they often climb to the top of a mountain or a high hill and leave their best blanket hanging upon a tree, as a gift to the Great Spirit. After a time they come again, and if it is gone, some other Indian or a white man having taken it, they think their gift has been accepted, and are very happy.

The feathers of the owl have a particular value, because they think these feathers strengthen their medicine, and make them like the owl—a bird which can see in the dark, and moves noiselessly, seeking its food after the other birds have folded their wings for the night. Otter skins, they think, impart to them the shrewdness of the otter. They are quick to notice the peculiarities of animals, and value them accordingly. When hunting, they scarcely ever kill a bear, a wolf or a lion, for these animals are bad medicine, and bring poor luck.

The name Absarokee (Crow), originated from the sparrow hawk. The Crows speak a dialect of their own and also have a method of making known their ideas by signs and gestures. The latter they use altogether when low-spirited or when traveling. The Crows, Sioux, Piegans, the Bloods and Gros Ventres, are properly Blackfeet Indians. Little quarrels have separated them, until they themselves scarcely know to what tribe their forefathers belonged, and historians are getting them badly confounded. These Crows stayed with us two days, and then started for the buffalo range on the dry fork of the Missouri River, to obtain their yearly supply of meat and robes.

Geese were valuable for their feathers in those days. Steward and I made a bargain with Mrs. Hoskins, to kill one hundred geese for her, at one dollar each. We thought we had the best of the bargain, as we felt sure we could kill that number in two days, or less, so we went down the river, and camped the first night near the water's edge, just above Pompey's pillar.

We were upon the road before it was fairly light the next morning, to take advantage of the early hours, when geese are flying about in greater numbers than at any other time of the day. We reached the mouth of Fly Creek in good time, stopped there two whole days, industriously hunting for geese, and killed but two, which we ate. The geese were unusually wild and saw us from afar. We were upon an island, and if we killed others, they were generally over the water and we could not get them.

"I'm a sucker if I ever hunt geese agin," said Steward. "It will do for boys in the States, but I'm going to the mountains."

CHAPTER XIV,

VARIOUS INTERESTING MATTERS—First kill bear—in a herd of buffalos—adventures with buffalo and mountain lion—something about Hiram Steward.

Upon one occasion when Steward and I had a contract to supply meat to Hoskins and McGirl, at Baker's battleground, our camp was situated on the headwaters of Razor Creek. For three days we had wandered around, through the foothills, looking for bears. The signs were plentiful, but we succeeded in getting only one bear, which Steward insisted upon calling a mongrel, and surely it was not of pure blood. We were returning to camp late in the evening, when we heard stones rattling down a bluff, and, pausing to listen, we saw a bear about two years old, of a yellowish brown color, climbing along the hillside.

In an instant, bang, bang, went our rifles and down he came with a roar. As he tumbled over, I gave him two more shots and he delivered up the ghost. We skinned him and Steward added the skin to his bedding. We arrived in camp, worn out with our day's tramp, and Steward fleshed his bear robe while I got supper. After a hearty meal we discussed the advisability of moving camp. We had been burning pitch-pine knots and my hair was so stiff it would scarcely bend, so I set about washing out the pitch. First I used bear's grease to cut the gum, then soap, with which I scrubbed and washed for half an hour, and quit in disgust, leaving it looking as though the calves had been sucking it, and in fact much worse than at first.

"Wall, Allen, you look purty now," laughingly said Steward, and he exclaimed: "Wall, I kalkerlate we will look higher in the mornin', as the bar is a high bird this time a year."

"All right," said I, "in the morning I will be ready to ascend."

Our camp was a little paradise. The green pines were dense as could be, and a beautiful cold spring of water was close at hand. The bunch grass was like a carpet. Nature had left nothing to be desired. Early the next morning, after a hearty breakfast, I shouldered my rifle and started up the mountain looking for my pony. After a long and tedious walk, I found his trail, and followed it over rocks, bad lands, logs and washouts. When I sat down to take a look from the top of the mountain, I saw the pony, grazing quietly, about half a mile away, and near him was an immense herd of buffaloes.

To get my horse and not scare the herd was the next procedure, so I went down the mountain until the buffaloes could not see me, then cut around the horse and found low ground, through which I crept, and finally made my way to him. When I had secured the horse, I found I had forgotten to bring a bridle or picket-rope, so I took a small strap, which I was using for suspenders, and buckled it on his lower jaw. I then proceeded to flank the buffaloes.

After a careful examination, I found the wind was opposite to the way I wished, for I had thought of running the herd toward camp, but I kept up my sneak until I was within one hundred and fifty yards, when I could see all sizes of the animals, calves, cows and bulls. I carefully filled my magazine, then was at a loss whether to kill one,

BUFFALO FEEDING IN THE YELLOWSTONE VALLEY.

mount the pony and give chase, or to mount and run them first.

My horse was a strange one to me as I had recently bought him. I recalled some of the great and splendid qualities which had been ascribed to him, but I did not believe much in them, so I decided to chase the buffaloes in the start as I knew I could shoot from his back. I placed the remaining cartridges in the front of my belt, readjusted my knife, mounted and started slowly toward the herd. I had gone about half the distance before they seemed to notice me, then an old bull gave a snort, threw up his tail, and started off like the wind.

The country was a high tableland about five miles wide between Razor Creek and the Musselshell River. The stampede of the immense herd made the ground shake. The earth was black before me, and the erected tails looked like the guns of an army. My horse gave one snort and darted toward the herd like an eagle on the wing. He came alongside an old bull almost instantly. In my excitement I dropped my strap and gave the bull a shot through the lungs, then another and again a third, when he gave a lunge and fell among his comrades, to be trampled into pieces.

The dust was flying like a cloud, and the sound of the galloping hoofs almost deafened me, but I caught sight of a fine, black cow, gave her a shot which broke her back, and down she went among the flying drove. I singled out a fine, two-year-old cow, drove two balls through her and she disappeared. I shot two calves and a four-year-old cow, and then found my cartridges were gone from the magazine. I soon filled it again, but only with hard work and by losing as many as I put in the gun. I was now completely surrounded by the herd and the dust was suffocating. My horse showed signs of giving out, so I took my gun in one hand and began to slap him on the side of the head, shooting everything that came near on the other side.

We crossed the head of a canyon, and such a crashing of old, dead pine and rattling over stones I have never heard since. My horse lost his footing once and fell. I thought I should be trampled to death, but the pony did not go clear down, and with one bound he went up the bank with the herd, in safety. I scarcely knew how or which way to turn to get out of the mass of flying brutes, but I did know that my situation was getting dangerous, so I turned to what I supposed to be the west.

My horse seemed to understand what I wanted, and soon got to an opening in the ranks, and was once more on open ground. I dismounted and watched the herd go by. Thousands of buffaloes passed and the roar sounded like thunder. I went to camp, covered with dust and perspiration, and Steward and I returned to the field of slaughter to find eighteen buffaloes, killed and wounded.

"Wall," said Steward, "that will do; we will make a winter camp here. This looks like livin'."

We skinned the choicest robes and took the meat to camp, which occupied us for three days. On the third morning, when we were coming in, I saw a large mountain lion, lying on a ledge of rocks, near where we had been passing. The old man straightened up in his saddle, pushed back his old white hat and said:

"Wall, you have had enough shooting lately. I will wait on his majesty."

He slid down from his jackass, pulled his old Sharp's from the sling and inserted a .44-75. He walked a few steps from the craggy ledge, raised his rifle as though he were going to shoot at a target, his right foot forward and his game leg under him. I thought he would never fire, but his arm was steady and the old reliable belched forth its compliments to the lion. A cloud of dust arose, just where the lion lay. He sprang to the ground, thirty feet below, and, giving a howl, started toward us with a foreleg broken. In an instant we both fired, but he came on faster, passing us to the right, when I gave him a broadsider which prostrated him. But he jumped up and bounded off again. Steward then gave him another ball which broke his back, and he dragged his hinder parts slowly down the hill, but soon died, as he had received several fatal shots. We left him lying there and went to camp, hung up our meat, skins and tongues, and then our camp was complete.

Hiram Steward told me much of his career in the Rocky Mountains, and I will record one incident which showed his fiery spirit. In the year 1878, late in the fall, many trappers and hunters had come, as usual, to the store of Hoskins and McGirl, for that firm was always ready to outfit a man, and to lend a helping hand to anyone who was deserving. Steward sat at one end of a card table and a man of Southern blood, named Jackson, at the other.

Gambling had taken a lull, and Steward took up a deck, and shuffled off the cards, saying "There's the red, there's the white and there's the blue." Jackson took this as an insult, sprang to his feet, saying he would not be insulted by any Yankee, drew his six-shooter, and called upon Steward to defend himself. Steward pulled open his old buckskin coat, set his slouched hat back on his head and his large, gray eyes flashed. Every one thought Jackson had run a successful bluff, when Steward stood up, and, without saying a word, walked behind the counter, grasped his old Sharp's and threw in a cartridge, saying:

"Jackson, I have not long to live and I know it. I am no shot with a six, but just come on and we will go over the river. I will shoot it out with you now. Come on."

All hands started to accompany them, and the crowd had gotten about half way down, when Jackson turned and went back to the store on the run. He never tried the bluff again, and was a laughing stock for all who had witnessed the affair.

CHAPTER XV.

On a bright September morning in the year 1878, Little Horn, the scout, came to my camp, and, after partaking of refreshment, invited me to smoke his peace pipe, and informed me that his heart was good. He then told me that he knew where the white man's money grew, for he had seen it in a mountain. He pointed to a gold ring which I wore upon my finger and said: "All the same as that."

Little Horn was a Bannock chief, thoroughly acquainted with all the surrounding country, as he had been roaming through the Rocky and the Big Horn mountains for ten years. I had hunted with him on several occasions, and, knowing him to be a truthful Indian, thought there might be something in his report. I was very busy drying deer hams, but told him I would go with him to this mountain in two sleeps if he wished. He was very much pleased and said we should go.

"Get heap money, buy heap ponies, have heap squaws." This was his idea of the pleasures which money can procure. He mounted his pony and galloped down the river, his blankets and long black hair flying in the air. Two days later he again made his appearance with two ponies, and a little bundle containing dried venison, and I was soon ready to accompany him.

After fording the Yellowstone we crossed the low ridges along Pryor Creek, passing many herds of deer, antelopes, elks, and small game of all kinds. About four o'clock in the afternoon we came to a clear, cool spring, where we dismounted, spread down our blankets, and prepared a lunch. While thus engaged we heard a noise, and, looking up, saw a large cinnamon bear coming down a little hill near by. Little Horn appeared to be greatly excited. He carried a Henry rifle, but he looked at it disdainfully, saying: "Heap no good *neputsa,* heap big gun, heap little."

I asked Little Horn to hold the horses, which allayed his fears, and I crept up the ravine until I was just below the bear. He was pulling down and eating the ripe fruit, and this he continued to do until he was within fifty feet of me. When I thought he was as close as I wished him, I gave a shrill whistle, and, as he raised himself up to look, I drew a fine bead for the butt of his ear and pulled. He gave a leap, rolled over, jumped upon his feet, and kept running round and round like a puppy after its tail, but finally paused, and I gave him one square in the head which put an end to further demonstrations. Little Horn came, took a good look at him and talking rapidly the while, said:

"White man heap good gun, heap big. Indian's gun heap too little."

The bear must have been engaged in a fight not very long since, for his skin was torn in half-a-dozen places, rendering it unfit for a robe; so we left him without depriving him of his ragged coat, finished our lunch and proceeded on our journey. When near the creek we saw a large otter (lutra canadensis) dive down the bank and take to the water. We leaped from our horses and gave chase. When he rose to the surface the Indian and I both fired, but overshot him. Down he went again and soon we saw him

DEADLOCK OF WHITE TAIL BUCKS.

Found in Judith Mountains.

swimming down the steam. The water at this point was about three feet deep but, as the animal went down the stream the water became shallow. When the otter got into water about twelve inches deep I shot at and wounded him slightly, which soon brought him to the surface and I finished the job.

Little Horn plunged in, brought out the otter, and, holding the little fellow high over his head, went through all the dances with which he was acquainted, saying: "Heap good medicine; Sioux no kill me now." I learned that he considered the otter the very best medicine known. The skins are worn on the Indians' hair, wound round their arms, fastened to their blankets, tied on their guns or saddles and on their ponies' tails. The chief was greatly delighted with the prize, which I had no desire to share with him.

The hour being late we camped under a large cottonwood, and our ponies enjoyed the rich grass which completely covered the ground. While getting supper I saw a fawn come out of some willows, about one hundred yards below us. I caught up my rifle and was raising it into position when a large buck came out, then came a doe followed by another fawn. They were all sleek and in good order, and were examining our camp. The Indian was under the cottonwood, too busy with his otter to notice what was going on. We had not killed much game, as we were prepared to carry very little, but I felt I should like a piece of the fawn, so I aimed at its shoulders and fired. The other deer jumped and so did the Indian, but the fawn wilted from the effects of cold lead, for the bullet broke both shoulders, and we soon had its liver broiling over the coals, and found the meat very palatable.

Supper over, I helped to skin the otter, and found it the toughest job I had ever undertaken, as every atom of the skin had to be cut from the flesh and only the very best knife would hold an edge. Little Horn stretched the skin around his head, allowing a large portion of it to form a graceful fold behind, and gave another exhibition of his war-dances. He related many incidents connected with his boyhood, spoke of the first Sioux ponies he had stolen, how he was followed by the owners and had killed one of their number, and how, when he reached his own tribe, they made a hero of him, dancing around the scalp and chanting his praises.

The young squaws all loved him after that, but he liked none so well as Pretty Nose, so he courted and married her. He dwelt with pleasure on the fact that a brave chief can have as many squaws as he can take care of, and I joined him in chanting their old "Ha, O, ha, ha, O." until he grew inexpressibly happy. We had no bedding except our saddle blankets, which were light, and as the night was cold, we were glad when morning dawned, that we might rise and stretch our chilled limbs before a blazing fire.

As we rode up the creek after breakfast the mountains seemed very near, but neverthless we were a long time in reaching them. At noon we stopped for refreshments and caught a fine mess of trout, which, with venison, constituted our bill of fare. We turned the horses' heads to the southwest and traveled through the main range. Upward we went through green, grassy parks, then down through the timber, walking for miles and leading our ponies.

As the twilight was gathering we reached a beautiful green spot, containing about twenty acres, all alive with elks. I think there must have been a thousand. I shot a fine calf and the others went crashing through the timber, crushing before them everything that would yield to their strength. Lying on our blankets beside a good fire, our ponies enjoying the bunch grass, we heard the murmuring of a little rivulet close by, mingled with the cry of coyotes, but the roar of a mountain lion, not far off, caused the ponies to huddle together like quail. The moon was full, the night calm, and the stars shone out like so many diamonds, glittering, dancing, and shooting in all directions.

The Indian, aroused from a peaceful slumber by the roaring of the lion, said: "Too close to *echetacasha* (river), we had better move." I told him it would be cowardly to run, and we could easily kill the lion if he came too close, but he replied, "Bad spirits travel at night and good spirits in the day."

More than an hour passed, when again the roaring was repeated, this time nearer and clearer than before. Little Horn, now thoroughly aroused, insisted upon moving, saying the lion would spring from the bushes to where we lay and devour us before we could make any defense. I said it would be his last spring if he attempted such a thing, and persuaded the Indian to lie down, by telling him that I had killed many lions and was not afraid of them. We were lying down with our clothes on, in order to be ready in case anything should happen; all was quiet once more and half an hour had passed when we heard the lion, softly creeping through the bushes like a cat.

Finally two fiery eyes looked through the foliage upon us, and slowly and cautiously he approached the carcass of the elk calf, weighing fully three hundred pounds and intact, except one leg which we had cut off. We expected he would go to tearing and eating the meat, but, to our amazement, he took the calf about the middle, raised it off the ground, and started off up the hill. The audacity of the act and the great strength displayed by the brute almost paralyzed me, but I resolved not to be robbed in that manner, right before my eyes, without offering any resistance, so, after seeing that Little Horn had his gun ready, I fired upon the robber. He let go of the calf and fell, but came toward us as fast as his broken hips would allow. Each of us gave him a shot, which struck him square in the chest, killing him almost instantly. He measured more than ten feet in length.

This danger being past we slept sweetly until morning, when I awoke to find myself alone. Filled with surprise I looked around for my companion, and saw a large grizzly bear covering the body of our rescued elk with leaves. I drew my rifle from under the blanket, when I was startled by a voice saying, "No shoot, he heap kill us both," and just below me, in a bush about ten feet high, I saw Little Horn, trying to screen himself from view.

I realized that we had very different game from elks or deer to deal with this time, and that our lives would probably pay the penalty, should the first shot not prove fatal. Besides the bear was on the up-hill side of us. This gave him a great advantage. I had once nearly lost my life in a similar position when attacking a grizzly and thought it might be advisable to let him alone and say nothing about the calf. Then the thought struck me that I had never yet weakened when called upon to rid the world of one of these brutes, and got behind a small pine tree, within thirty yards of him.

As I watched the powerful beast tearing up the earth as a covering for the calf, I thought of climbing the tree before shooting, but the idea seemed so ridiculous that it was soon abandoned. I gave the customary whistle, and, when all was ready, took sight intending to sever his jugular vein, if possible. The sight blurred before I got ready to pull, he changed his position and the ball broke his lower jaw only, passing on through his nose. He made a bound toward me and I sprang up the tree without loss of time. What a howl he uttered as he came toward the tree, passed on over our bed and almost through the fire. He struck the bush which sheltered Little Horn and almost shook him from his perch.

Like an infuriated bull he went flying down the mountains, evidently as blind as a bat, and when he reached the precipice, he stumbled over into the water below. I found the Indian still in his bush, looking like a superannuated ghost, so great was his superstitious dread of bears. I coaxed him down, and, his fears having subsided, he said: "Bear crazy, heap no good." After breakfast we walked over to the precipice to view the remains of the grizzly, and he lay there in the gorge below, stone dead.

Wending our way through forests of pine, over hills and rocks, I became exhausted and was heartily regretting this fruitless journey, when my companion called my attention to a high mountain which overlooks the Big Horn canyon, and said that was the mountain where the money grew. I had visited the place before and was sure nothing was to be found there except some base metal in the quartz. It seemed that we would never reach the top of the mountain, but when we did, it looked as though all the game in the Northwest had congregated to celebrate our coming.

We rounded a narrow ledge which overhung the river, so high above it that the roar of the rapids could not be heard, and the river, thousands of feet below, looked like a silver thread. About fifty yards in front of us stood a mountain ram with the largest pair of horns I had ever seen, and it was for these that I shot him through the heart. In his death struggles, however, he managed to kick himself off the shelf and fell into the abyss below, robbing me of the prize I so much coveted.

We found some fine specimens of silver and copper, but the gold turned out to be a delusion, so we turned our heads homeward, wiser, if not richer men. Little Horn was sadly disappointed as his ponies and squaws must be relinquished, at least for the present. When we arrived at the home, he took his otter skin, bade me "How," and I have never seen him since.

CHAPTER XVI.

Starting up Fly Creek, we rode fast all day through the warm sun, and about noon of the next day, we were near the Big Horn mountains. What a scene lay before us. The verdant hills were covered with hundreds of buffaloes. The sunshine lent luster to their black glossy coats. The calves were at play, running here and there over the grassy slopes. This was not the only picture we looked upon that day. Small herds of antelopes dotted the hills both on the right and left, their white sides glimmering in the distance. The valleys were occupied by elks and antelopes, while, far away near the foothills, strolled a large band of elks, that had just descended from the heights above, to enjoy the grass and warmth of the valley. Nothing could have been added to improve the picture. Men never designed anything half so lovely. Many a hunter of to-day would give much to see the like. All was silent, save that now and then the clear notes of the lark broke the stillness. We let the animals graze, while we sat upon a knoll to feast our eyes. I was trembling from head to foot with contending emotions. I wanted to try my skill with a rifle, yet did not wish to mar the peaceful scene.

"What's the matter with you?" Steward asked. "Did you never see a buffalo before, or are you skeered."

"I am charmed with the buffaloes, elks, antelopes, hills, valleys, and mountains."

"Whar is the elk?" he asked in surprise, straining his failing eyes to see them.

"Look among the foothills to the north and you will see plenty of them," I said.

"Oh, yes, I see them now. Wal, I guess we will be able to load our packs soon."

"We must first find wood and water, then we will take a promenade over that way. Let's be off at once. I am eager for the chase."

Steward needed no further urging. We took our course toward a quaking-asp thicket, about two miles to the northwest. We there found plenty of wood and water. The pack-saddles, blankets, and cooking utensils were torn from the backs of our weary animals, but they kept looking into the thicket, snorting and acting very strangely.

"I'll bet thar's Injuns in thar," said Steward, with a wise shake of his head. "Old John always tells me when thar's Injuns nigh."

"I'll take a turn through the thicket and see what's up, while you picket the horses," I said.

I took my gun and went around the thicket, looking closely, but could find no trail of any kind. I came back and reported to Steward, but he shook his head dubiously.

"John don't lie," he said decidedly. "Go into the hollar and look. Thar's a screw loose somewhar. Keep your hand on your head if you value your scalp."

I took an old game trail and soon saw the tracks of a very large bear. My senses were alert at once; I filled my gun with cartridges and crept forward more carefully. A

large hole torn through the fallen pea and hop vines arrested
my attention.   I raised the hammer of my gun and started
to crawl in upon my hands and knees.   I followed the opening about thirty yards, and was within ten yards of the opposite bank, when his bearship gave a growl that made me
think I had business outside; I did not fly exactly, but bade
him a hasty adieu, crawling out much faster than I entered.
When I got out to where the air was not so oppressive, I
took shelter behind a tree.   I attempted to coax the brute out
by throwing stones, but failed.   Every means was tried in
vain.   He still refused to leave his vantage-ground.   The
vines were so dense that I could not see to get a shot at him
and, if I ventured in again, he might take me unawares and
make a meal of me.   In my dilemma I called to Steward that
I had run a monstrous rat to earth, and needed assistance.
He lost no time in coming and appeared upon the opposite
side, with his old Sharp's across his shoulder and his knife
swinging from his belt.

"It's a bar instead of Injuns?" he called to me in a
questioning tone.

"Yes," I replied, "and you are not far from him; just
around that little bank, under those vines, is his castle."

"How do you know?" he asked.

"I was fool enough to crawl in until he gave me to
understand my company was not agreeable."

"Wal, I'll soon find him out.   He can't run no bluff on
me; if I had an explosive ball, I'd jist walk down thar and
blow him inside out."

"Try the torpedo racket on him," I said.

"I have a torpedo in old 'reliable' that I'll try on him,"
said Steward.

The bear acted as though he both heard and understood
our talk, for at that moment he scattered the vines and ut-

5

tered savage growls which made me turn cold. Before
Steward could fire, the bear was close upon him, but a ball
from the rifle struck the brute in the heart while he was
crossing a log which gave way, throwing Bruin over backward. Steward put in another cartridge and snapped it,
but it did not explode. By this time the bear had regained
his feet, and, maddened with rage, was rushing at Steward,
who had extracted the shell of the bad cartridge, but not the
ball, which stuck fast in the grooves of his rifle. It was
a terrible position for a defenseless man, having the bear almost upon him, while, from my position on the other side,
I could see only the top of Steward's head, for he was close
to the vines and I could not know how the battle was going,
although the sounds told me much. I knew my presence was
required, but was undecided whether to force my way
through the undergrowth, or run around. Either course
would have consumed valuable time. Steward intimated
what was best for me to do, by dropping his gun and starting up hill, as fast as his lame leg would allow him. I decided to remain perched upon the rock where I was, with
the hope that I might get a shot at the bear. Steward rushed
up hill, the bear close behind, in plain sight now. Steward's
buckskin coat, which was covered with blood, hair, grease,
and all kinds of filth, stood out straight behind him. I could
not get a shot for fear of hitting him, and began to think
he was doomed to be devoured alive.

I called out at the top of my voice, "Run for the rock up
hill. Hurry, he is almost on your back."

Steward reboubled his sped and went as I directed him,
the bear gaining upon him so fast that I felt sure it would
catch him before he could find safely upon the rock. My
time for action was come. I sent a ball through the tops of
the bushes, which took effect in the shoulder of the bear.

DR. ALLEN'S SUCCESSFUL SHOT.

The Bear That Caused Stewart's Death.

He stopped for a moment, roaring with pain and twisting his head to get at the wound; but started again in pursuit of poor Steward. I fired a second time, just as the brute was getting ready to strip the buckskin coat from Steward's back, but did not stop the animal. A thrill of horror ran through me at the thought of what must speedly occur if something was not done to stay the bear. I nerved myself, with great effort, and fired at its head, just as Steward made a leap to grasp the edge of the rock. He caught it, but the frail brink broke and let him down. Luckily for him, however, my last shot had struck the bear in the neck and had broken the spinal cord and they fell together at the same moment.

I could hardly find courage to look. The bear in its deathstruggle did not forget Steward, but caught the old man by the waistband of his elk-skin pantaloons, and threw him twenty feet down the hill. The fearful cry that escaped the lips of Steward as he was tossed through the air unnerved me. I tore through the brush, across the hollow and up the hill. Steward lay motionless, to all appearances lifeless. I feared the bear was not quite dead, and gave it another ball to make sure. The report caused Steward to stir feebly. I examined him carefully and found no marks of violence upon him, but his eyes were encircled by a yellow band, often seen in the face of the dead. I filled my hat with water and bathed his face, which revived him slowly, and looking wildly around, his eyes fell upon the dead bear.

"How did I git away from him?" he asked in a low, feeble voice, a gleam of intelligence lighting up his face.

"He threw you down hill because he did not like your company any better than mine," I replied.

I raised him to a sitting posture. He remained in a profound silence for a time, evidently going through the late adventure in his mind. Finally he said with a great solemnity of manner:

"Great God! Twenty-five years in the mountains, and that's the closest call I ever had yit."

"You are not dead yet," I said, "and you are good for twenty-five years more."

Steward never got over the terrible shock and fright of this affair. It preyed upon his mind continually, his hitherto robust constitution failed soon after. He died alone, in his cabin on Pryor Creek, and his body was found by a hunter two or three days thereafter. Little was known of his previous history, but he told me once, that he had been married in the East and that family troubles had driven him to the mountains to seek peace of mind. It is needless to say that the adventure with the bear terminated our hunt, so I skinned the animal and got one hundred and seventy-six pounds of oil out of the carcass. It was the largest bear I ever saw. The hide was fully nine feet square, just as it was stripped from the body.

I met John Len, an old hunter and trapper, at Benson's Landing, where we made up a party of five and started up Mission Creek to hunt white-tailed deer. Our first camp was at the old Indian agency, which consisted of a church, several framed houses and a few adobe buildings. The place would have been entirely deserted, but for the presence of one half-breed and his deaf and dumb squaw. The next morning we drove to the canyon, where we established our headquarters. The little stream was full of trout, and we congratulated ourselves that if other game failed us, the trout would do. After dinner we wandered off in different directions, wherever our individual fancies led us, in search of game. I traveled through ravines and over mountain sides, until I was tired, and then sat upon a log to rest.

The body tires from walking in this mountainous country, but the eye never wearies of the prospect. Suddenly a rifle-shot broke in upon my meditations, and a deer came down the creek with the speed of an arrow. I imitated the cry of a deer, and fired when he paused. He was never to race over the hills again, and floundered out into the creek, but I took him by the horns, brought him to shore, and, in a very few minutes, he was hanging in quarters on the limbs of a tree. When I got to camp, I found that my deer was the only game killed that day, so we soon brought it in, and had a good supper.

The usual number of stories, wild and improbable, were told that night around the camp-fire. Every hunter who has been out with a number of others, knows what a pleasant pastime story-telling is after a hard day's march, and how often it is kept up for the greater part of the night. When we started out the next day, we adopted our plan of the day before, each taking a different route. I went far up the stream, and half-way up the mountain-side, where I found myself in a nice little park. In the farther end was a large five-pronged buck, waiting for a ball from my rifle. I raised the sights to three hundred yards, took careful aim at his breast, and let fly. He sprang into the air, switched his tail, bucked like a broncho and went off like a shot, tearing away the bushes that lay in his path. I stepped off the distance from where I had stood to where he had been and I found that I had miscalculated the distance, as it was four hundred yards. The blood that he had shed was of a light red color, proving the wound to be trifling. I followed him for about a mile along the mountainside, missed the trail, gave him up for lost, and started for camp. On the way I met one of the boys, also returning, with his half-breed shepherd and wolfdog, Captain Jinks.

We walked leisurely along, chatting together, taking no particular notice of anything, until the movements of the dog ahead, told us he was following a trail. We stopped to investigate. There were deer tracks, but all along there was a round hole in the earth, in one of the tracks. We followed down the stream as fast as our feet could find the ground; the dog was by this time out of sight among the bushes, but his cries broke upon our ears.

"Captain Jinks is at bay," Jack said, "and we will have some fun."

Half a mile farther brought us to a little opening, through which we saw a deer, with horns down, jumping at the dog. When we were within fifty yards, the deer saw us and thought it policy to run. This was not so easily done, for the cliff before it was one hundred feet high, and nearly perpendicular. The dog was not willing to give up the fight, especially as help was near, and caught the deer by the ham, just as it reached the foot of the cliff.

Over went dog and deer in a close embrace, that we feared would crush the life out of the dog. But no! the struggle was renewed with so much vigor that both rolled into the river with a loud splash. The deer could wade, but the dog must swim or drown. Every time the dog tried to climb the bank, the deer jumped at him and sent him back into the water. If ever a dog's face wore a pitiful, pleading expression, it was that of Captain Jinks, when he looked at us after the performance had been repeated several times, and he was almost worn out.

I thought it time to interfere in behalf of the faithful dog, and brought down the deer with one shot. His heavy body fell back into the water with a loud splash, turning its clear color to a crimson red in his vicinity, the water boiling around him as he struggled with his feet and legs. Jack went down by a circuitous route and pulled his almost drowned dog out of the water. Together we landed the deer, and, as the camp was only about one hundred yards below, we managed to take him there without help.

It was the same deer that I had wounded in the park, by breaking his leg low down. The holes we noticed among the tracks were made by the broken bone sticking into the ground as he bounded along. Six deer were killed that day. The boys (excepting Len and myself) were satisfied with the trip and the amount of game killed, and went back to the Landing the next morning, but we mounted our ponies and started for Boulder Creek, where we were sure to find plenty of game.

Night found us on a summit of a mountain, where we laid out our route for the morrow and followed it when morning dawned. While crossing a low divide, we saw seven large bull elks coming along the ridge toward us. We hastily dismounted, guessed the distance at four hundred yards and shot at a large elk, which drew up its back a little, and the entire band started off at their utmost speed. We followed in the same manner and found the bull lying dead, not more than three hundred yards from where we shot him, the ball having pierced his heart. We dressed him, piled his head and hams upon a rock, and went on again. As the sun was sinking to rest, we reached Middle Boulder Creek and followed a narrow trail, making four short angles, that led up to a dense growth of cottonwoods. There was a narrow path into the grove, and we were both surprised and pleased to find an old shack in the clearing, secure from prying eyes. It was just the place where one might live without being troubled by Indians, and no doubt was chosen with that object in view. There was also a stable adjoining the shack, large enough for six or eight ponies. The place was deserted, and there were no traces to lead us to suppose any human being had been there for a long time. It seemed designed by Providence for our special use. Our scanty stock of provisions was soon unpacked, and we cooked supper in our new house.

After a good night's rest and a hearty breakfast, we were in the best of spirits, and set out—John going down and I up the stream. Several coveys of grouse started up at my approach, but I did not want to frighten larger game for the sake of grouse. Suddenly ten deer came out of a dense cottonwood thicket on my right, so noiselessly and orderly as to scarcely disturb a leaf or twig. Their heads were held erect, their long slender necks were finely arched, their eyes were standing out like stars on a clear, frosty night.

Two bucks, side by side, led the way, while a large stag with ponderous horns brought up the rear, with the does and fawns between. I shot at the stag. The report echoed and reechoed from the mountain to mountain and vibrated through the valley. The deer swept along with the speed of birds on the wing, and were soon lost among the low hills, but the old stag made a few jumps, then came to earth, with his glossy coat bathed in blood.

About three miles farther I saw something out in the water that looked like a beaver on a cake of ice. I went as close to it as possible and saw that the animal was an otter. He was eating something that I could not make out, and a shot in the eye laid him on his back. There is always more than one way of doing a thing, so I brought him to the shore with a long hooked pole, for the ice would not bear my weight. He was a large male. By him lay a fine trout, half eaten. I examined his stomach, and found it overloaded with trout.

About noon I came to a singular little stream, that I called the Devil's Slide; the stream was very narrow; its banks at this point were solid, perpendicular rocks, sixty feet high. The water was rushing through this slide with the rapidity of an arrow. Farther on it disappeared in the recesses of the rocks, where it was lost for a short distance, but it raised again, after the rocks were passed, and flowed gently upward. It was a curious freak of nature, and I gazed upon it until the descending sun warned me to retrace my steps.

I had gone but a short distance when a skunk stepped boldly into my path, and, forgetting his manners, refused to give the road. This made me angry and the battle commenced. Small stones went whizzing through the air, and my opponent was getting the worst of the battle, when a large grizzly bear appeared upon the scene. She came out of a patch of bushes just beyond the skunk, and stood upon her haunches, looking me over with an air that seemed to forbid further hostilities. There was no tree near, but a high rock offered shelter in case I should need it. I thought I could easily break her neck, but she did not change her position, so I sent a ball at her just as she started to get down on all fours. The ball struck her in the back of the neck, making only a flesh wound. She roared as only a grizzly can roar and make a lunge at me. I ran for the rock, but found that I could not climb it. I then rushed around it and toward the creek, hoping to escape that way. The dodge gave me time to throw in another cartridge, and, as the bear came around the rock, I gave her another ball in in the breast. A roar loud and long rent the air, and, before I had time to turn, she was almost upon me. I then ran for dear life, imagining all the time that I could feel her sharp claws and teeth tearing my flesh. She was a knowing brute, and, instead of following in the rear as she rounded the rock, she headed off my retreat.

There was nothing that could be done, but to turn
aside and jump into the creek. With one desperate leap I
cleared the ice that lay along the bank, and fell into the running water. I was a fast swimmer and got some start of
her, but she soon gained upon me rapidly. A large rock was
upon the opposite bank, some distance down the stream.
My only hope lay in reaching it. Horror! I had not
thought of the Devil's Slide, and was almost into the rapids
that would dash me to death against the rocks.

Death menaced me on every hand. I threw my side
against the waves, and ventured on a little further. The
rapids were not so near as I thought, although the waves
were strong. One last powerful stroke brought me to shore
a little way below the rock, but, while climbing the step
bank, the big brute came so near, that I was compelled to
relinquish my grasp and push her off with my gun. Con-
centrating all of my strength, I pushed her with so much
force as to send her out into the rapids, which bore her to
speedy destruction.

Had it been possible to live in the boiling waters, the
tall rocks on either side made it impossible for her to get out,
and I ran down the bank, trying to catch a glimpse of her
but in vain. I was almost ready to die with cold and fatigue.
My wet clothes hung upon me like leaden weights. In this
condition I reached camp, made a fire, dried my clothes,
cooking supper at the same time. A strong cup of coffee
strengthened and relieved me at once. John was still on the
war-path, or had been downed by a grizzly.

The waning light shone dimly through large cracks in
the wall, for darkness was settling around the shack. The
sweet, yet mournful, murmur of the stream fell soothingly
upon my wearied senses. I could hear the deer as they
crossed and recrossed and the beavers slapping the water

with their tails repeatedly, while over all sounded the lonely cry of the owl. The snapping of dry sticks aroused me from a semi-conscious state, and I saw a large bull elk dash through the brush and across the creek before I could get my gun. His eyes like two jack lamps as he passed.

John came up through the willows just then, and, after a warm supper, we stretched our weary limbs before the fire and recounted the adventures of the day. John had killed three deer, and I told him of my deer and the skunk, but paused to take breath before I mentioned the bear.

"But what makes you look so lank?" he inquired? "Your clothes fit you closer than they did when we started out."

"Only a swimming race with a grizzly. You should have seen me when it was over," I said. We had a big laugh after all was told, but I assure you that I did not even smile while the performance was going on.

We then laid out the next day's work, which was a hunt far up the stream. By daylight we were upon our ponies, cantering toward the mountains with all of our effects. Large numbers of grouse, eagles, hawks, antelopes, and deer were seen, but we pressed onward for the canyon, reaching it about noon. While we were looking for a camping-place, a band of mountain sheep came rushing down the precipice, rolling stones and logs before them. Our pack-animals were very much frightened, and reared and plunged wildly. The saddle-horses acted but little better, and the shots we fired missed their marks, because our horses would not stand still a moment. There were no trees to which to tie the animals, but I finally fastened mine to a heavy log, and, dropping upon one knee, sent a ball after the leader. He fell, and I made eight more shots, killing three sheep. The pack-horses that carried our provisions came back without his load. We looked around, found the flour, salt, pepper, coffee and other eatables scattered over the ground ; so we had nothing left to eat but straight sheep.

We started for home the next morning, but were delayed two days by high waters. We stopped to pick up the game we had killed at different places along the road. A bald eagle was taking care of our elk on the divide, tearing its flesh and picking out its eyes. Wolves had evidently been there also, for there was but one arm left.

We made our camp that night high on the mountainside, and, as darkness came on, the wind rose, and the air was very cold. In the night I awoke to find myself wet with perspiration, and almost smothered by some heavy thing, I could not tell what. I raised the covering, and found we were under about ten inches of snow. We had some trouble in getting a fire started, but finally succeeded and prepared a light breakfast. We were not far from home, but John, fearing to cross the high waters, went up the river to find a better crossing, while I took the shortest way.

I arrived at the river in the afternoon and tied my meat to the end of a long rope, then mounted my pony and pulled my load after me, letting out the rope as it was needed. The load nearly took my pony down stream, but he was a good swimmer, and carried me safely to the other shore, where some of the other boys were cheering me. I was soon eating a hearty supper, relating my adventures at the same time.

A COUGAR OR MOUNTAIN LION.

CHAPTER XVII.

The pleasures of the hunt are more than half due to the companions who accompany me, but hunting alone has its advantages. There is no one to stand by and ridicule when you miss your aim, or to tell how much better he could have done if you had given him a chance. Failing to find any one who was ready and willing, at that particular time, to lay by other work to chase deer wherever they might be found, I started up Pryor Creek, with three horses, but on the mission before mentioned.

The waters of this creek are very clear and full of trout as it flows from the mountains; but, as it nears the Yellowstone, several small tributaries come in from the Bad Lands, making the water dark and muddy, and catfish in large numbers take the place of the trout. A hard day's drive, from early morn until sundown, brought me near the canyon, where I feasted from a fawn, killed on the way, and potatoes and coffee. Then I sought repose, and did not awaken until the sun was high in the heavens next day.

When the canyon was reached I made camp, picketed my horses, shouldered my rifle, and took to the hills, longing to get within shot of deer or elk. The country around was very broken; but, by climbing rocks and holding on to bushes,

I managed to keep upon my feet until exhausted. Finally I was compelled to sit down upon a rock for a few moments' rest. Deep-cut canyons, filled with dark green pines, surrounded by massive walls of gray granite, were yawning in the broad noonday light.

A bald eagle, looking as if perched on air, was high above me in the heavens, sailing with pinions spread, while not a quiver or motion of his body was perceptible. As though he would fain express his scorn for a creature so far beneath him, he looked down upon me. Suddenly he bent his body earthward, clapped his wings close to his sides, and came down within one hundred yards. Around and around me he sailed, apparently contemplating the advisability of descending upon me. He paused over my head, scanning the rocks upon which I sat, taking in my position before he should gather me in his talons. The temptation to conquer this proud bird was too strong to be resisted. The power which held him in space was quickly terminated by a ball from my rifle, and he fell to the earth with a force that split his body in twain.

The effects produced by a single rifle-shot in an unhabited region are wonderful. While the report was echoing from canyon to canyon, ravens screamed, the mountain thrush chattered in his tree, while the squirrels scampered from branch to branch, frisking their tails and chattering in chorus. All were intent upon seeing the intruder and determining what was meant by the unusual commotion. A large bull elk, either fearing for his own safety or curious to learn the cause of the disturbance, came rushing up the canyon, tearing through the small trees and bushes with his horns as he leaped through the air. Anxious to convert him into meat for my own use, I gave him a hasty shot. Alas! he heeded not the summons, but increased his speed, leaving a trail of blood to mark his course.

I followed, as fast as fallen trees and other obstructions would permit, for about two miles, when, covered with blood and foam, he started up from behind a fallen tree. Again the report of my rifle rang through the air, and the animal reeled, fell, and lay prostrate upon the ground, the blood flowing in a stream from his neck. It was no small job to cut him up, but I finally succeeded in securing his hams, and was starting for the ponies, when a terrible roar caused me to look in the direction whence it came.

I saw a large grizzly coming, as fast as it could, to help me dispose of my game, and probably to dispose of me, should I deny its right to a share of the elk. Two cubs brought up the rear, eagerly following the trail of blood, their savage appetites fully aroused. My first impulse was to climb a tree, but the idea of relinquishing my game to these blood-thirsty animals was not to be considered, so I fired at the foremost cub, and had the satisfaction of seeing it drop dead. The mother paused a moment to bewail the loss of her offspring, only to see the other stretched lifeless beside the first.

I now directed a shot at her ear, but missed the mark and slightly fractured her lower jaw. She immediately deserted her dead cubs and rushed at me like a tornado, uttering fierce growls. Another shot, intended for the head, struck her in the neck, and with a deafening roar she leaped toward me. I attempted to fire again, but she was too quick for me and knocked the rifle from my hands. At the same instant I jumped behind a small tree and swung myself up among its branches.

Vain were her attempts to dislodge me. Her wounds distracted her attention, and, at last, faint from loss of blood, she lay down. I threw stick after stick at her, hoping to drive her to a location more pleasing to myself, but she only rolled her fiery eyes, uttering low guttural growls, until death came to her release. Fearing she might be "playing 'possum," I hurled my knife at her with all my force. Yes, she was certainly dead! Still my hair would stand on end and my teeth chatter, as I stepped down from my retreat, grasped my gun, and put another ball into her, just to make assurance doubly sure.

The spark of life was not quite extinct, but she struggled only for a moment. Tired and somewhat ruffled in temper, I sat down to take in the situation. The earth was torn up in several places, and the grass, but an hour ago so green and beautiful, was dyed with blood. After indulging in a long reverie. I looked around for one of the cubs that was missing, and found it dead in a thicket with an ugly hole through its back.

The sun was casting its last rays upon the mountain sides when I started for camp, worn out with the recent battle. Being anxious to reach camp before darkness should overtake me, I decided to follow the creek, though it led me through brush and over logs, and necessitated my wading its waters, which were very swift. Passing through a deep cut in the creek bottom, fenced in by high smooth walls, I caught sight of a large pair of elk's antlers on my right. Upon making a closer examination, I found thirteen pairs of antlers, besides other bones all within a short distance, and the animals had evidently been killed recently, for flesh still clung to the bones.

At this point there was a deep recess in the rocky wall, forming a cave about sixty feet in width by twelve in length. There was a wide entrance at the farther end, running into the mountain, large enough to admit any animal. While noting the appearance of this cave, which I termed in my mind the cave of death, or the home of beasts of prey, a little clod came tumbling down from overhead and, looking up quickly, I saw a large mountain lion, with eyes gleaming, his tail swinging, as was his custom when getting ready for a leap. None too soon I sent a ball on its massion, and beheld him drop dead in front of his lair.

Pressing still farther into the cave, I found a full-grown elk lying dead, and from fifteen to twenty pairs of antlers close to the mouth of the den.   There were, besides, the heads of mountain sheep and carcasses of antelopes.   Some of the horns were badly decayed, showing that the work of destruction had been going on for a long time. Others looked fresh, and the animals had evidently been the victims of mountain lions.

This kind of lion is from eight to eleven feet in length, low in stature, having powerful limbs, and jaws capable of tearing into pieces almost any animal.   They secure their game in much the same manner as the Indian practices warfare; by either lying in ambush or crouched upon a rock in the shadow of a tree over some watering-place or mountain pass, and, while their victims are refreshing themselves, or passing quickly from one district to another, they leap upon them with a force which crushes them to the earth, never to rise again.   They seldom attack man unless wounded.

The shortest road to camp proved to be the longest, so long did I linger by the way, and it was almost dark when I reached that most desirable of all spots to the tired hunter. But my hunger was soon appeased, and ere long I was far away in dreamland.

Very early next morning I saddled my ponies and set out to bring in my game.   The ponies could not be induced to go near the carcess of the bear, so I tied them up and first went to take care of the elk.   What a sight to meet the gaze of a hungry man!   The elk had been torn to pieces and nicely

DEAD LOCK OF WHITE TAIL BUCKS FOUND IN JUDITH MOUNTAINS.

covered up for future use, and the bear had likewise met with rough usage; her coat was almost torn from her back, and the cubs had entirely disappeared. Yesterday's work had been in vain. My treasures were gone, and, with a sad heart, I left the remains to the prowling thieves that had despoiled me.

Going down a ridge, covered with green grass and dotted here and there by trees, I saw a deer standing by a rock about one hundred yards distant.

"I shall not go to camp empty-handed if I can help it," I remarked to myself, as I hastily dismounted, tied the ponies to a bush, and took deliberate aim. The deer made one bound and fell dead. He was as beautiful a specimen of his kind as I had ever seen, so I packed him on one of the ponies and made a fresh start.

Nothing else particularly attracted my attention until I had gone several miles beyond, when my ponies gave a snort and rushed madly to one side.

A large bear had started up from a clump of bushes and ran like mad. Two of the ponies got loose and left me far behind, and the rearing of the one I rode made it impossible for me to get a shot. After a long chase, I came up with the pack-ponies and found the deer swinging beneath them. That night I dined on venison, potatoes, onions, warm biscuits, and coffee. Sitting by a blazing fire, I went through the events of the day in imagination.

While engaged in getting the meat ready for the journey home, darkness came down in what seemed an incredibly short space of time. While preparing to rest upon my bed of saddle-blankets, I heard the splash of waters, and, looking up the creek, saw two fiery eyes approaching. I noiselessly took up my gun, fired, and the flash lighted up the darkness several yards in all directions; then came a terrible splash, and the blazing orbs drew nearer. I had taken the precaution of throwing a cartridge into the magazine immediately after firing, and it was well that I did, for a wounded elk came dashing toward my fire, furious with pain. His large antlers glittered in the firelight, while the blood flowing from a wound over his face made him truly an object of pity, as well as of fear. I fired again. He gave a great lunge and fell almost into the fire. The ponies were in a terrible fright, rearing and plunging, but the pins held them fast. Another streak of luck after the disappointment of the morning. I went to bed well satisfied with the success of the day, congratulating myself upon the amount of meat in store, and on the next morning by daylight was on the road, loaded with the best of game.

In this manner the time passed, fall came, and I began to tire of my hunter's life. My mind dwelt upon my home in Ohio and I had a desire to see my old friends once more, so I commenced preparations for a homeward journey.

CHAPTER XVIII.

It was November. Leaves of purple and gold covered
all the land and the bare branches of the trees waved to and
fro in the winds, which swept in fitful gusts through the
camp of a party of Crow Indians on the Little Horn River.
The braves had just returned from a successful hunt, their
ponies loaded with the choicest of meats and buffalo robes.
The joyous songs of the dusky maids rang through the air
as the young bucks deposited at their feet the fruits of the
chase, and the older squaws crowded around the warriors,
exhibiting every token of the warmest welcome.

The more bashful maids were anxiously awaiting the
approach of their sweethearts, the custom being for each one
to take his load of meat to the tepee of the maid he loves, that
she may select the choicest cuts before leaving the bulk with
his parents. The papooses were running, and jumping, and
screaming, and dogs innumerable swelled the chorus.

It was on this day that my sixteen-foot skiff, which I
had been working at for some time, was finished, stored full
of necessaries, and ready to sail. The canvas was set upright on the rear end, to form a sort of tent, that could be
lowered if the weather demanded. While the hubbub was
at its height in the Indian camp, I launched my skiff into

the crystal waters of the Litttle Horn, attended by the
"Hows" and good wishes of the chiefs. I was starting for
my home, a journey of about twelve hundred miles, and
must travel a good part of the way, alone in my little boat,
through an Indian country. With one oar I pushed the craft
from the bank and was soon floating down with the current.

The news had gone through the camp that the big
medicine-man was going to the rising sun in the little *mar-
shey* (boat), and as I guided slowly away, the bank was alive
with reds of all sexes, sizes, and ages. Old Raw Hide was
the last person my eyes rested upon, as my skiff rounded
the bend in the river, and he shouted after me, that I would
get through all right if I would remember to be very quiet
and careful while passing through the Sioux, who were
camped somewhere on the river.

At this season of the year the waters of the Little Horn
are very low, so in some places it was hard pulling, but
when I reached the Big Horn I had fair sailing, for its
waters were swift and deep. When once fairly afloat, my
light skiff whirled like a cork, but, with a few strokes, 1
set it straight in the current and dashed along at the will of
the restless tide. White gulls floated through the air and
skimmed the surface of the waves with their downy breasts,
while their chattering notes continually reminded me of
their presence. My thoughts were far away. My mind
wandered back to the old home, where relatives and friends
were still plodding along in the same old way, the same old
round of duty stretching from day to day, leading them
onward through the year.

I took a brief retrospective view of the hardships and
dangers through which I had passed—many hunts, many
camp-scenes, and, more than all, I thought of the brave boys
who had given up their lives on the plains. So vividly did

the past rise up before me, that I fancied I could hear the tramp of the war-horses, and the savage yells of the Sioux as they charged upon us. I remembered friendships, made and cemented under trying circumstances, that will last as long as life itself.

My reverie was terminated by the sight of a large beaver swimming rapidly before me. All instincts of a hunter were at once aroused within me, though the game was very small. I was about fifty yards from him when he made a dive. I had been drifting idly along, but now I caught the oars, made several rapid strokes, and dropped them again when close upon him. He arose, dived again and I repeated the rowing process. This time I came out ahead of him. His house was evidently below me, and when he next came to the surface, almost drowned, I took deliberate aim at the back of his head and fired. I reached the spot where he had last appeared, and there was plenty of hair, blood, and brains visible, but no beaver; he had gone down never to rise gain. I could only thank him for diverting my mind from thoughts that had become painful.

Although the day had been warm, as the sun declined, and night drew near, the air became quite cold. I had traveled a long distance, was hungry, tired and cold, so I rode to a beautiful island, which I found covered with tall trees, red willows and bilberry bushes, forming a thick undergrowth. Hauling my skiff out upon a little sandbar, I soon had a fire with coffee simmering over it. A slight noise in the bushes, some distance below, caught my ear, and, with gun in hand, I pushed in that direction to discover its cause. My eyes were gladdened by the sight of a large doe and two fawns, going to the water's edge to drink. I decided to secure the fawn next to me, and brought him down at one shot. The others turned and fled across the island, making the bushes rattle in their flight.

I broiled a fine steak over the coals, and, in addition, with my meal I had cranberry sauce, fried potatoes and warm biscuits. As I had eaten no dinner, I did each dish full justice. I then attempted to spend a quiet hour in reading by the fire, but beavers splashing the water and the running of deer kept me constantly on the alert, however much I tried to disregard them. At ten o'clock I spread my bed in the skiff and laid down to pleasant dreams, with no fear of danger.

Before the sun had risen, I was awakened by a great noise in the bushes, and, on looking out, saw a bear with the forequarters of my fawn. Nothing so enrages me as to behold the impudent manner in which this animal invariably pounces upon and carries off another's property. I gave him a shot near the heart, and my best wishes went with it. He started to run. I gave him another in the hind parts; then he reared, roared, and tore up the bushes in his path as far as I could see him.

Concluding that he could not live to make so free with another's property, I lay down and took another nap. After I had arisen, five deer came bounding past; and I caught up my gun through force of habit, but, reflecting that I had no room for more meat nor time to attend to it, I allowed them to pass unmolested, and made another start toward my destination.

At the lower end of the island I discovered an object which, as I approached, grew larger and larger, but it was not until I was very close that I saw it was the bear I had shot in the morning, lying with his legs straight up in the air, his countenance wearing that look of ferocity habitual to the grizzly, even in death. Leaving him to the mercy of wild beasts, I pushed on to the Yellowstone. Wild geese and ducks frequently came very close, but, as time was precious, I gave them no heed.

But why undertake to follow each day's adventures? It would prove both wearisome and uninteresting, though to myself, without companionship, each little incident seemed fraught with peculiar meaning.   The days, so far, had been pleasant, but the nights were growing colder and colder, and I greatly feared a snow would fall, or the river would freeze over, which would leave me in a very bad situation, as the voyage would have to be discontinued until warm weather.   I reached the Yellowstone River on the second day, a distance of seventy-five miles from my starting point, and was now making my way toward the Missouri.

When these fears began to oppress my mind, I redoubled my diligence, and on the third night stopped upon a gravel-bar, beneath some giant cottonwood trees, where the cool breezes seemed unusually refreshing.   After a hearty supper, I saw a large herd of antelopes coming down the opposite hillside—it was not yet dark—so I let my skiff bear me along until I was hidden from their view, when I rowed rapidly toward the point for which they were making, until only a small hill intervened between me and the game. They had reached the river and were drinking.   I could not see them from where I stood, and concluded that they had scented me and gone back, but I found the trail and started toward the river.   Suddenly they appeared, having satisfied their thirst, and came rushing toward me like the wind, their nimble feet scattering the gravel in every direction, and throwing it high into the air.   While they were passing me, I brought down three of their number, helped myself to as much of their flesh as I could well carry, and settled down for the night.

My boat was now heavily loaded, but she was well built, and, the water being deep, I had no difficulty in pulling her through as rapidly as my strength, which was not inconsiderable, would permit. I was resting for a moment, when I chanced to look down the river, and saw, on a small island, as many as one hundred buffaloes. Some were lying down, others standing gazing idly around, while some of them were goring the bank with their horns.

As my boat was drifting directly toward them, I made no other movement than to take up my gun, which was supported by hooks at my side. The wind, which was blowing toward me, was favorable. They did not so much as turn their heads, and, should they discover me, they might easily mistake my skiff for a floating tree. When the report of my rifle broke the stillness, they started up and were off, their languor instantly forsaking them, being succeeded by the wildest alarm.

When they rushed into the stream, such a great volume of water was thrown into the air that it seemed as if the river were lifted from its bed. The waves, lashed into white caps, receded before the mass of living, struggling creatures, like surging billows before a mighty tempest. Finally they took to swimming quietly, when I pulled rapidly toward them and fired another volley of shots, when those in the rear leaped upon those just in front, a large number being submerged and great confusion ensued. They were all heaped together, some riding upon others which were almost drowned.

I came close enough to punch one with an oar, but when he turned for fight the current was too much for him. He gave up the attempt and made for the bank, where a general stampede took place. Some went one way and some another, uttering loud snorts. They kept up a gallop, across the valley, as far as I could see them. The excitement of the chase lent me fresh strength and again I pushed forward. I could have killed a score or more of them had I so desired.

The next day I saw game in the distance, running as though in fright, and this gave me some uneasiness, as I suspected Indians to be in the vicinity—perhaps the bloodthirsty Sioux, against whom I had been warned. I began making all preparations in my power to make, in case of an attack, and arranged my bundles of robes to be used as breastworks. A few miles farther on many Indian tepees could be seen in a large body of timber along the river. I soon discovered the Indians were Crows, and, much relieved, I approached them without hesitation. The warriors seemed to be holding a troubled council.

Attracted by my boat, warriors, squaws and papooses assembled on the river bank, all crying out, "How! how!" A little girl crawled out to the end of a log, extending far over the water, and sat there, her bead-like eyes glistening like diamonds, while her guardians seemed to have no fears for her safety. I secured my boat and soon learned that their gloomy looks were caused by a rumor that a large party of Sioux were coming from the south, and they feared they would steal their ponies, even if no further harm were intended.

A number of squaws gathered around me and asked where I was going. I replied that I was going to the great Father of Waters, beyond the rising sun. They said my boat was too small to sail in such great waters, but I assured them the Great Spirit was with me, which statement excited a general laugh, one making bold to say that I would lose my scalp before I got through the Sioux country. I distributed some trifling gifts among them and bade them farewell. An old chief hallooed after me, to say if I saw any Indians without tepees, I might know they were Sioux.

About ten o'clock next day, as I was urging my boat through a rough rapid, I saw about four hundred yards ahead of me as many as five hundred Indians crossing the river. I fired three shots from my Winchester after them, just to give them a scare. The balls struck almost at the same time. Such a fright as they caused! The stolen horses were rushed through the water and some of the colts were nearly drowned. One of the Indians lost a red blanket, but would not stop to pick it up.

When they reached land they went like the wind, never once looking behind them. I gave them a few more shots, none of which did any injury, and they must have thought that a large body of the enemy was after them. They were soon winding through the foothills and out of sight. I boarded my man-of-war, sent her down the rapids like an arrow, and picked up the red blanket, which is still among my possessions, a valued relic.

When night approached, the snow began to fall and the wind to blow. I kept on my way, not knowing where I should land, until finally I reached a place where the waters made such a fearful roar that I feared there might be rapids ahead, and, unwilling to take any chances, I pulled for the shore. I found a large cottonwood, to which I tied my boat, and was trying to make out my location in the darkness, when two dogs came rushing upon me with the ferocity of hungry wolves. I drew my gun, and they halted just in time to save their hides from being perforated. A cabin door opened, and a long, lean man came out, calling:

"Here Tiger! Here Tiger!"

"Halloo!" said I.

"Halloo, stranger! Where in the dickens did you come from? I've jest come in from a scouting expedition, and did not know there was a white man in the country. Come in; git out, you dogs!"

I followed him into the cabin, where the feeble rays

of a tallow candle were extinguished by a blast of wind through the open door. "Git a seat, and I'll strike a light," called out my host, in what seemed to be a familiar voice, and, in fact, I felt sure that I had heard it before. The candle being relighted, he turned to inspect his guest, and immediately burst out with:

"Holy angels, Allen! Why, old boy! Well, I never!"

"Archie McInerty!" I replied. "The only time we ever met, we were both of us on the first grand jury that ever sat in Miles City, and here we meet again."

"Sit down! sit down!" he said, in a commanding tone of voice. "I'll git some supper, and then we'll talk over old times."

In a short time he had prepared a repast that I can taste even yet in my imagination, so delicious was it to my palate after that hard day's work. We ate and talked for more than two hours, relating our past experiences. Archie is an old-timer on the Yellowstone, has passed through many places, and is truly a genuine hunter.

Next morning I bade him adieu, and started out on what proved to be the most disagreeable day of my journey. An east wind bore heavily against me, and when night came I was almost exhausted. When I attempted to rise from my bed next morning, I thought some one must be holding me down; but, on pushing back the canvass, I saw that I was buried beneath the snow, which had fallen to the depth of six inches.

The wind, although somewhat moderated, impeded my progress as much as it had the day previous. I pulled hard all day, and was surprised to find that I had made no more than fifteen miles. My boat was weakening, for it had been almost torn to pieces against the rocks in Buffalo Rapids, and several times I feared she would go no farther. The water was at its lowest mark, and the sharp rocks had given her some fearful knocks.

As she was half full of water, I was obliged to stop for repairs, and fortunately I had with me a bucket of pitch, which saved me from walking the rest of the way. I was out of fresh meat, and resolved to get a supply. About noon a large mountain sheep came toward the river, then another and still another appeared; so I selected a fine young lamb, and was soon packing it away in the boat.

Near Glendive I met a party of hunters, some of whom I had seen before, while others were known to me by reputation. When I arrived at Fort Buford, the old steamer Mc-Cloud was getting ready to make her last trip for that season. Gladly I quitted my frail craft and took cabin passage for Bismarck, well protected from the inclemency of the weather. Never mortal man felt happier than I at that time. For thirteen days I had been battling with wind and waves, exposed to many dangers, and with no companion to cheer me on the way.

We made the trip from Fort Buford to Bismarck in four days. When I boarded the railroad train I was wearing my buckskin suit, which made me an object of no little curiosity and remark to the Eastern people, who, perhaps, regarded me as at least half savage. When my home station was reached, I stopped at a hotel and barely escaped being refused the privilege of the house, owing to my appearance. But, after convincing the landlord that I was born of civilized parents, in the state of Ohio, he consented to let me remain. With a good team and driver, the fourteen miles to my home were soon passed, and at last I found myself again among friends.

CHAPTER XIX.

I had returned to civilization surfeited with wild Western life. I was determined to settle down in my old home and enjoy the many privileges and advantages from which frontiersmen are debarred. But I could not feel that it was the same old home I had so fondly and often remembered during my wanderings. Or rather, I was not the same man that I had been when I left those familiar scenes, and the simple pleasures that once so delighted me had now become tasteless. The sight of a fence was disagreeable, after having looked so long across boundless prairies, whose beauty the hand of man had not yet marred. I longed for the old free life, for a sight of the dear old mountains, and, after a short stay, I again made my way westward, landing at Fort Custer, Montana.

For a time I enjoyed life among the soldiers there stationed in the garrison. But, the weather being fine, I craved for a good hunt, and, through the kindness of Captain Fowler, then acting quartermaster, I obtained five pack mules and a good saddle-horse. In company with Mike Barrett, a first-class packer, and taking with us plenty of rations, ammunition and supplies, I crossed the Big Horn ferry and started for Bovia Creek, twenty miles distant. On the road we killed a few grouse and jack-rabbits, the only game that came within rifle-shot. We went into camp early, in order to unpack and look around a little, lay our plans, and be ready to commence operations in earnest in the morning.

Bovia Creek rises in the Pryor mountains and empties into the Big Horn River. The country around was then a favorable location for hunters. While here in camp nothing transpired worth relating, and we went on to Clark's Creek, remained over night, and from there packed to the Yellowstone, where we camped on Canyon Creek. Here we spent several days looking around, and then, with I. W. Danford and Frank Somers, fresh recruits and both good shots, we started in quest of game.

We forded the Yellowstone, and had traveled southward about five miles, when we ran into a band of deer and opened up a lively fire upon them, which soon diminished their numbers. We dressed fourteen and hung them up for the magpies to feast on while we rode on to Pryor Creek. The grass had been burned off, and, as plenty of grazing space is a necessity to a hunting party with animals to be fed, we almost despaired of finding a camping-place until we reached a small island, containing about one acre of ground well covered with grass.

"There is not a bite of meat in camp," said Somers, as we prepared supper.

The mules appeared to be very uneasy. With ears thrown forward, they kept looking into a patch of cherry-bushes. Remembering several occasions upon which mules had scented game and thus revealed its presence, I took my rifle and went into the bushes, where my suspicions were verified. A deer bounded out of the patch and ran toward the creek. I fired when he was almost across the stream. The ball struck the ground in front of him, throwing up

SOME BLACK-TAILED DOES.

In the Canyon.

a cloud of dust, which caused him to turn toward me, when I ran broadside and fired again, breaking his neck.

"Plenty of meat in camp now," I said, and we soon had some steaks for supper. The boys had caught a few trout, but it was too late in the day for successful fishing.

The next day, after a hard ride far up the mountain, we camped near a little rill, whose clear, cold waters bubbled from beneath massive rocks. I was in advance of the boys and started up three white-tailed deer. One fell at the first shot, but the other two turned and were running across the hill when I killed the second, and, by a lucky shot dispatched the third, as he was nearing the hilltop. This was the first time I had been able to kill three of these deer at three shots, and my success caused me to smile a little. It is harder to kill three white-tailed deer than a dozen others, for they do not stop to see where the balls are coming from, but bound off at their utmost speed.

We took these deer safely to camp and made another trip up the canyon. This time we encountered a large deer with four fawns. The deer was killed by the first shot. The report of the gun greatly alarmed the fawns, and they strove hard to get out of our reach, but we soon had all of them down. Here we separated, each man taking a different route, and I went up the main canyon to where it widened to its greatest breadth. I reached the top of a hill that looked down into a quaking-asp thicket and commenced rolling stones into it. This had the desired effect, a crashing noise was heard, and out came ten deer, their eyes distended with fright. I leveled my gun at the largest. He gave a few jumps up hill and fell dead. I then shot another large doe. By this time they saw where I was, and ran from, instead of toward, me, but I kept on shooting until I had killed two more and wounded another. I was so completely satis-

6

fied with sport that I did not follow the other deer any farther, but contentedly cared for the meat. When I told Mike what I had done, he rolled up his eyes and exclaimed:

"I never knew you could shoot at all. I don't believe half you have said. Give it to me light."

I finally persuaded him to go with me, taking with us two mules and an ax to cut a good road. He called one of the mules Jack, the other Antelope. We gathered up the game, packed it on Jack and Antelope, and started back, Mike leading the way and I following. When we reached a steep bank where the trail was very narrow, the mules began to crowd, and in other ways to exhibit their mulish nature, until Antelope lost his footing and fell into the water on his back.

Mike warmed the old fellow up with a brush vigorously applied; but Antelope was too heavily loaded to get up without assistance. We relieved him of his load, finally pulling him out of the water, but we had a hard trip to camp, tearing through thorns and beaver-dams. There were now sixteen deer dressed and ready to be taken home.

When I awoke the next morning, a large deer was standing above the camp looking down upon us. The report of a shot from my rifle set the camp in an uproar. The deer came crashing toward us, and fell dead within fifty yards of camp. After a splendid breakfast, we packed our venison and separated, Mike and I going to Custer, Frank and Danford to their homes on Canyon Creek.

Traveling along beneath the broiling sun, Mike and I became very thirsty, and our mules were also suffering for a cooling draught, when we noticed some bushes and found that they fringed the banks of a little rivulet. With cries which rivaled the demonstrations made by the children of Israel in the wilderness under similar circumstances, we were joyfully approaching the stream when we saw a fawn's head rise above the grass.   I leaped from my saddle, but Mike forestalled me, and sent a ball crashing through the animal's heart just as it rose to its feet.   Another deer jumped from the grass, and I shot it through the neck. Then we all drank from the stream until our thirst was sated. Afterward we journeyed on through the Bad Lands, over hills and streams, frequently running on to game for which we had no use, as we lacked the means for its transportation.

After dark we struck our old camp on Bovia Creek, where the coyotes, which had been following us for miles, were joined by others, and the band set up such a howling that we could not hear each other talk.   After they had quieted down, wolves took up the refrain, which was kept up until far into the night.   Next morning we found them still lingering near and gave a chase, killing four of the whelps, just to get satisfaction for the loss of sleep we had sustained.

After we had moved out, from the top of a little knoll we saw as many as twenty more of the beasts.   I fired into the mob, and such squalling and scattering as there was there I have seldom seen.   They went like feathers before a gale.

We met a party of twenty Indians, and had quite a conversation with them about hunting, killing bears and shooting other wild animals.   They give bears, lions and rattlesnakes a wide berth.   When we arrived at Custer we presented one of the finest of the fawns to Captain Fowler, and the other deer were distributed among the people.

Three weeks later I received an invitation to go on a fishing excursion on the upper Big Horn, which I was not slow in accepting, and, in two days' time, our party was catching whitefish by the dozen.

One morning I took a good saddle-horse and started up the mountain, determined to have some sport of a more exciting nature. An old wagon track took me into a thickly wooded gulch, and I soon found myself surrounded by such a mass of rugged rocks that I could go no farther, so I turned back to find a trail that would lead up the mountain. Three times I attempted to ascend the broken ledge of rocks which overhung the pine trees. At length I saw a large elk's trail which wound around the mountain, like a huge serpent, as far as the eye could see. I led my pony slowly up this steep and rugged road, until the valley below looked like a mere speck, the winding river glittered like a silver thread, and the green trees looked no taller than blades of grass.

From the top of the mountain I beheld the Rocky Mountains in the west, the Crazys to the north and the long sawtooth ranges of the Big Horn in the south. Deep down in the canyon of the Big Horn mountains the waters, which had fallen thousands of feet, rolled over huge rocks, and the foam and white caps showed what a struggle was going on between the boulders and the rushing tide. So far was I above the mighty conflict that only a dull, low roar reached my ears.

I gathered some stones and hurled them into the chasm. Not a sound arose from its depths, and mountain sheep standing near the water's edge paid no attention. Far below in a clump of cherry bushes were five deer, gathering and eating the ripe fruit, while several bands of elk were idly wandering, all unconscious of danger. While viewing the scene in all its beauty, the desire to shoot something became so strong that I could not resist the impulse, and I pulled trigger on a large sheep, which stood upon a rock fully one thousand feet below me on the opposite side of the river.

I saw no sign that the ball had struck the ground, neither did the sheep stir. I tried again with like results. I then raised the rear sight to one thousand yards and the ball struck within thirty feet of him. When the sight was raised to eleven hundred yards the bullet landed directly under his body, causing him to leap from the rock. I made several further attempts simply as experiments, for I could not have reached the sheep had I killed him.

I prepared and ate a lunch, then followed the canyon about five miles up the main range, whence, with a good pair of glasses I could see a large part of Wyoming and Idaho. Suddenly a sharp peal of thunder warned me that a storm was brewing. The heavens above were as clear as a bell, but far in the distance dark clouds were rising, while the lightning was shooting its forked shafts in every direction. The clouds came rolling along the sides of the mountains, apparently swallowing up everything in their path, a violent gust of wind sweeping wildly before them. No need now to wonder where the storm was coming from, nor where it would spend its fury. Trees were torn up by the roots and hurled into the canyon below, and game fled in all directions to places of safety.

Protected from the storm by a huge rock, I looked calmly upon the scene of destruction. A band of sheep, leaping from rock to rock, came directly toward me and I shot at one but the gale befriended it. The mountains appeared to be on fire, so vivid and continuous was the lightning. I would that I could portray the grandeur of the spectacle, which will ever remain stamped upon my memory. The storm having spent itself, I picketed my horse and lay down to rest, for it would have been impossible to have found my way to camp through the darkness, and the greater part of the night was passed in watching the lightning playing through the heavens.

When I awoke the clouds had gathered thicker than on the evening before, while a dense fog covered the mountains. I began retracing my way, but could make little headway, frequently running nearly into game that would climb the rocks with a terrible noise. When almost ready to give up and camp where I was, until I should be able to see my way, to my great joy the darkness and fog gave way to a burst of sunshine, and I soon found myself again in the valley.

The boys had suffered much anxiety on my account and welcomed me back to camp. The evening was passed in my relating an account of the storm in the mountains. Long strings of trout garnished our camp, so I had no need to ask what their success had been during my absence. After dinner the next day we pulled out, each man having gained some fresh experience, which could not fail to interest the folks at home.

Winter was almost over and the genial rays of the sun fell upon the earth, giving promise of delightful days to come. The white sides of the antelopes rendered them everywhere conspicuous, as they lazily passed to and fro, nipping the wild sage. A few scattering flocks of wild geese were to be seen against the blue sky. Their "honk, honk," alone broke the quiet, which to me seemed almost overpowering, as the little "jerkey,' loaded with United States mail, the driver and myself, hastened to the next station on the opposite side of the river. This station (a mere hole in the ground) was kept by Old Major, as everyone called him. We knew no other name for the man, nor did we know anything of his history, excepting that he had earned his title in the volunteer service and had been discharged for drunkenness.

We were trying hard to reach the station in time for

dinner but could not, as we had to cross the river, which showed signs of breaking up, the ice being open in several places. About three o'clock in the afternoon we reached the crossing place, near Pompey's Pillar, and found the Major out looking for a safe place for us to cross. I held the team while the Major and the driver surveyed the ice with troubled looks.

"Come right away here; I find a place vot is shust as goot as never vas!" called out the Major.

"Be careful!" I said; "don't get so close to that air hole or you will get your clothes wet."

"Oh no, I vill not, it ist youst as stout as any poddy. Come right here; mind the bonies und you go quick across."

Just then the Major sank through the soft ice. The current was about to take him under when he stuck up one of his legs, caught on the ice and held himself there until we pulled him out. The old man was nearly gone and the water ran out of his mouth, while he staggered like a drunken man. He went home to change his wet garments and we finally succeeded in crossing, a short distance above.

Major, none the worse for his bath, was busy preparing supper as we drove up. He had boiled the ham of a buffalo calf for two days, over an old kiln which he had made outside the dugout, until it resembled soup. He told us that the fresh team we expected to find awaiting us had broken loose, and had been gone all day. He had gone after the horses but had only seen some large wild animals.

Frank started out to find the missing team, and by dint of much questioning, I drew out the old man and made him confess that he had not been after the horses at all, but had seen the yellow dogs from a little knoll just above his house. I tried to persuade him to show me where they made their appearance but he would not move an inch. He indicated a certain point of rocks and said they had a den there. I started to look for the horses in another direction and soon found them in a large ravine.

Coming back by the point of rocks mentioned, I saw about half of the carcass of a deer lying near, which led me to make a closer investigation. Next I found a large mountain ram, to all appearance just killed, with its heart eaten out. A large opening strewn with bones was in the rocks and these indications plainly proved the nature of the yellow dogs seen there. I sat down under a fir tree, upon a large rock, waiting until some of the animals should make their appearance.

Sleep had almost overpowered me when a low roar called me to my senses. I looked around and on the rocks, one hundred feet above me, was a yellow dog, in the shape of the largest female lion I had ever seen. She was crouched upon a shelf, from which she had been watching me for I know not how long. Her low cry had the desired effect, for in a moment two others, both males, appeared at her side. They seemed to feel that danger was at hand, for they lashed their tails from one side to the other, apparently holding council.

I was filled with the desire to slay these three beasts. I filled the magazine of my Winchester, took a careful view of the surroundings, and singled out one of the males, as he stood broadside to me, writhing his tail like a serpent. I drew a bead on his heart and fired. With a fearful bound he came down head first, uttering terrible howls and cries, and landed within fifty feet of where I stood. He raised himself for a leap, but a shot just under the right eye settled him forever. The others sneaked into a large hole on the top of the ledge.

Quiet being restored, a young lion thought it safe to

venture out of the den at the foot of the rocks, to see what had happened. This one did resemble a yellow dog and I laughed aloud as I recalled the Major's description. I shot him fairly between the eyes and one ball was sufficient. Again I sat down and waited. All was still, so I got up and looked around, taking care not to get too close while the fierce old female still lived. No more lions appeared, but fresh proofs of their destructive powers met my eyes.

When I returned, I found a large herd of buffaloes drinking within one hundred yards of the Major's dugout. I shot a fine two-year-old, which gave a plunge forward, stood still a moment, then began to stagger and fell dead. Major was in ecstacies at the prospect of so much meat. The herd crossed the river and disappeared at once. Major was soon cutting and carving away at his buffalo, and such a mess of blood, hairs and dirt as he presented I never saw before. I finally took pity on him and helped him cut away the hams, telling him at the same time all about my sport with his yellow dogs. He was anxious to see them but refused to accompany me to the spot, his fear and dread being too great.

Having nothing particular to do only to follow my inclinations, I determined to revisit the den and wait for further developments. I seated myself on the same rock I had before occupied, straining my eyes in a vain effort to penetrate the darkness that filled the entrance of this den of wild beasts. Soon a young lion stalked forth, viewing the surroundings with a suspicious air, but I restrained the impulse to shoot as I was anxious to secure the old one. A slight noise, directly behind and below me, called my attention and there was the old female within thirty feet of me. She was in a crouching position, her ears lying close to her neck, her long, slim tail moving from side to side in a threatening manner.

She had no hostile intentions at that moment, but was getting ready to leap into a tree, and from that point of vantage to avoid open war if possible. I aimed to give her a ball between the eyes, and, when the crack of my rifle broke the silence, I heard a thud, and could see that she had sprung toward the tree, but had not been able to reach the coveted position. Through the smoke I gave her another hasty shot which broke her back, but did not deter her from making a desperate effort to reach me.

I found a long stick and thrust it into her mouth, and chewing it into fragments seemed to afford some relief to her wrath. I then sought for the young lion but he had taken warning and was not to be seen. Now that I had nothing to fear from the female, I approached the den boldly. It seemed to consist of two compartments. The one above being a watching-place or lookout, while the lower served for a home or resting place, and was strewn with bones of all kinds, which were sickening to behold.

The old Major was delighted when I related to him my adventure. He said he was so much afraid of the animals he could scarcely get any sleep at night, that they sometimes roared in a manner that made him tremble in his boots, and he would be glad to know they were all killed.

Toward evening I set out once more and this time prevailed upon the Major to accompany me. We made our way very carefully toward the fir tree near which the three lions lay dead. When the Major saw them his eyes were distended until they resembled full moons, and he showed a disposition to take to his heels. We had not been there long before the young lion appeared and the old man yelled out at the top of his voice. The aroused lion started to run, but a ball from my rifle caught him in the hip, causing a deep roar of pain.

Major started up a tree, as lively as a cat, not remembering that the lion could climb too. I fired at the animal again as it was entering the den, but think I overshot. We now made a general survey of the field of carnage, congratulating ourselves upon the good work done. We poisoned the carcasses of a large sheep and of a deer for the benefit of the survivors, if there were any, and left the point of rocks untenanted by its former bloodthirsty inhabitants.

As I had a week in which to reach the point for which I had started, I was in no hurry to leave the game, which was plentiful here, or the Major, who was a capital story teller. His stories were mostly of incidents connected with his own life, which had been strange and eventful. About seven o'clock that night, the little "jerkey," which was to bear me on my journey, came rattling up to the door. We passed a very pleasant evening together, the Major giving the driver a full account of our victory over the yellow dogs. Early the next morning we started out on our further way. The river bottoms were covered with buffaloes and antelopes, and the country was appropriately termed the "Indian's paradise." After a hard day's drive, swimming streams, etc., we arrived, completely exhausted at the old camp below, where Miles City now stands.

CHAPTER XX.

Buffalo v. Bear—A Strange Contest.

Once as I was returning from a trip to some mines, or supposed mines (which had been reported rich in gold, but upon examination had proved to be worthless), and was crossing a low range in the big mountains west of Rotten Grass, my almost exhausted pony suddenly recovered his animation and sniffed the air repeatedly. Being very much fatigued, I gave no heed to his demonstrations, but pushed on a few steps farther, where a clear, running spring invited me to dismount. Soon both horse and rider were eagerly drinking from the same fountain. I fastened the pony with a lariat, removed the saddle from his tired back and left him cropping the rich bunch grass with evident relish, while I began to prepare my own repast.

Soon I heard a snorting, and, hastening toward my pony, found the former strange behavior repeated with an increased energy and a great show of fear. I looked around, could see nothing, so I returned and finished my meal, took a bath in the water and was looking over my small pack, when my pony again ran toward me in great fright. I then took my rifle and walked rapidly in the direction whence his look said he apprehended danger, and about four hundred yards away I saw a dozen buffaloes, quietly grazing near some quaking asps.

I crept up as close as I could without disturbing them, and had selected a fat calf for my victim, when a full-grown bull came tearing out of the bushes and ran toward the herd. I did not know how to account for this strange freak, and I saw him looking in the direction from which he came, shaking his ponderous head in an angry manner. Only a short time was given me to wonder what would happen next, when a full-sized grizzly bounded out after the bull and rushed toward the herd.

The cows began to form a circle, while the calves were rushing wildly around. The latter were quickly surrounded by the cows, thus keeping the little fellows on the inside, as is the custom of the buffaloes when danger threatens. The bull took up his position in the rear, with a manner which indicated his determination to protect the females and their young, with his life if necessary. It was soon evident that some of the herd would become a meal for his bearship, unless they acted immediately in their own defense.

The bull saw just how matters stood, and, when the bear was almost at his heels, turned swiftly and met bruin as a mountain ram meets his antagonist. They came together with a thud, which fairly stunned them both, and they rebounded from the concussion like balls, and paused for an instant to recover from the shock. The bear then made a fresh start for the herd, but was again confronted by the bull.

The bear seemed to understand fully the motives which actuated his opponent, so he raised upon his haunches, and prepared to do battle with the bull, before he made another attempt to secure a fresh young calf. At that moment the bull lowered his head, shot forward with his tail standing straight in the air, and struck the bear full in the stomach. The bear in turn caught him around the neck and proceeded to tear the flesh from his shoulders, while the bull gave the grizzly some terrible wounds with his horns, and he finally made a desperate charge which compelled the bear to relinquish his hold, when the buffalo ran over his body and attempted to join the herd.

Wild with the rage, the bear quickly regained his footing, pursued and overtook the bull, who then turned like a flash and gave him another charge. This time bruin sprang upon the buffalo's back, and fastened his claws and teeth in the great fellow's flesh, a surprise for which the bull was not prepared. But he was equal to the situation and showed no small skill as an imitator of the bronco bucker. The buffalo plunged first one way, then the other, while the bear held on with a death-like grip, until it also was surprised by the bull's turning a complete somersault. Before the bear could recover the bull was upon it with his feet, and buried his horns deep in its shoulder. The bear then dealt the bison a blow with its paw, which sounded far off and made the bull shake his head with pain.

All this time the herd stood awaiting orders from their leader, and, whenever there was a lull in the battle, he glanced anxiously toward them. The bear was now deeply wounded in the shoulder. The bull was fearfully mangled about the neck. The blood flowed freely from both, while great bunches of hair were scattered in every direction. The bear now made a leap for the bull's back, but was caught between the fore-legs on the horns of the latter and received a terrible wound. It was then thrown upon its back and the bull plunged over it, goring it the while with his sharp horns.

The bear seized the opportunity to catch its enemy in the flank, tearing off a great mouthful of hide, but the bull turned and jumped upon it with both fore-feet and gave the animal another wound. The bear then caught his antagonist

DEATH BATTLE OF BUFFALO AND GRIZZLY BEAR.

by the back of the neck and they rolled over together. They were now in the wildest state of excitement, both suffering severe pain, each looking like a great mass of animated sand and blood. They started apart and stood within twenty feet of each other, panting like race-horses. The bear's mouth was full of hair and blood, while the bull's horns were red with gore for more than half their length, showing how deeply they had penetrated the body of the bear.

They stood apart but a few moments. The bull kept glancing toward his little family, while the bear approached one step at a time and raised itself on its hind legs, preparing to renew the conflict. I could hardly keep myself from sending a ball through the bear's worthless body, for I found myself in sympathy with the bull from the first, but I was curious to see how the affair would terminate. The battle had carried them closer and closer to the herd, and a two-year-old bull, seeing how matters stood with his defender, and burning with the desire to test his own strength, came upon the scene, pawed the ground, bowed his back, and rushed upon the bear with all his force, but was repulsed with a blow on the side of his head that turned him half-way round.

His old friend was close at hand, however, and taking advantage of the situation gave the bear another goring. The young bull kept shaking his head the while. The blow he had received had evidently stunned him, but he walked up within a few yards of the bear, turned himself sidewise, took a few steps, then flew again at his antagonist, plunged his horns into its bowels, making a gaping wound that allowed part of the entrails to fall out. Maddened with pain, the infuriated bear caught him by the hump with its claws, and tore the flesh from the back of the youngster's neck with his teeth, leaving the bones bare. The little bull roared as though imploring mercy, while the old one came again to his rescue and struck bruin a heavy blow in the back.

I now began to feel sorry for the grizzly, as he could no longer raise himself upon his haunches, and so I gave the old bull a shot through the heart, just as he was making another charge upon his fallen foe. The bear paid no attention to the shot, but seemed determined to have satisfaction out of his remaining enemy, though the young bull seemed willing to give up the struggle and depart in peace, taking warning perhaps from the fate of his friend.

Picking himself up as best he could, bruin made another attack, dealing the young buffalo a blow on the top of its head which staggered it. The bear now lay upon his back a mass of gore, evidently dying, and the bull had received a blow from which he could not recover. I then walked up close to them, and out of sympathy shot the bear through the brain. The bull was still standing, throwing his head up and down, the blood pouring from his nose and ears, so I released him from an existence which had certainly become unendurable, and saw him stagger and fall over the body of the bear.

This was one of the bloodiest battles between animals I have ever witnessed, and was maintained on both sides with equal courage and determination. The combatants had fought with all the strength and ferocity of their savage natures. "He who fights and runs away may live to fight another day." Animals seldom possess this element of cowardice when contending for their rights, or when satisfying the demands of appetite. I stood looking upon the remains until my heart grew sick within me, then mounted my faithful pony, and was soon flying down the valley.

At nightfall I drew rein near the spot where Fort Smith used to stand, refreshed myself with a few mouthfuls of supper, and turned in on my saddle blankets for the night, under the sheltering boughs of a large cottonwood. The roar of the waters, the rustling of leaves, the cries of coyotes and the howling of wolves, robbed me of sleep and made me feel that the infernal regions could not be very far off. I fired two or three shots in a vain attempt to frighten the brutes into silence, then built a fire and lay down to rest but not to sleep. I reached Fort Custer by noon the next day, having had no adventure worth relating, save the battle I had witnessed.

CHAPTER XXI.

THE AMERICAN GAZELLE.—A LAST BATTLE.

The family of fan-tail deer (gazella dorcas) which once inhabited the great Northwest, and the whole Rocky Mountain region, has gradually disappeared, and to-day there is scarcely a vestige left to remind one of the little groups that were seen so frequently, twenty years ago, along the streams and in the foothills. Little has been written about them, but careful observers have found some of the skeletons and tiny horns, which, in many instances, have passed for those of small white-tail deer.

But old-timers, who were more intimately acquainted with them, and who have often seen them in the far-off jungles where they retired to raise their young, cannot be so mistaken. There, away from the lion and other enemies, was the nursery for the gazelles, of whose large brown eyes the poets love to sing. Such haunts are unapproachable to animals of prey without giving sufficient warning to the mother, whose eyes and ears are ever alert.

These deer or gazelles, resemble in color the white-tail, or Virginia deer, turning from brownish gray in winter to a reddish brown in summer. Their stomachs and throats are white, and they are from two to two and one-half feet high at the shoulders. The tail is almost eighteen inches in length, and when erect and spread out, it is nearly six inches wide and resembles a large fan. When running slowly, they twist

HORNS OF FAN-TAILED DEER (GAZELLE).
Now Extinct.

AN OTTER FISHING.

their tails from side to side nervously, and keep looking back on the trail.   But, when once satisfied of real danger, they are considered almost the fleetest animals to be found in the mountains.

At times, they range along the streams with the white-tail deer and again they are in the mountains, with those of the black-tail family. The young have white spots along their sides and little black or brown spots on their throats, which disappear when they are grown.   The males have tiny horns like the white-tail deer, with one curved antler.   The points grow out of this main antler and stand up straight.   The two main beams incline together, but never fork, as do those of the black-tail deer.

The hoof is broad at the heel, quite pointed at the toe. The head of the female is almost like that of a fox, broad at the ears, tapering to a sharp point at the nose.   I doubt very much if one were ever killed by a sportsman after looking into its pleading eyes, so full of tender emotion, and of that magnetic charm, known only to those who have often met wild animals on mountain and plain.

With the vanishing buffalo went also the beautiful gazelle, and to-day the grandeur of mountain and valley is bereft of their charming presence, leaving a lack which cannot be supplied.   Even the few sad relics of bones and horns will soon have reverted to the earth, whence they sprang.

On the bank of the Seven Blackfoot, which extends between the Musselshell and the Missouri rivers, lies a country as wild now as when its savage tribes joined there in scalp dances in the seventeenth century.   The country was shattered by volcanic eruptions long before the advent of the savages, at the time when the mastodon roamed this unknown region, and where bisons, mountain sheep, bears, cougars, deer, and elks still stalk abroad.   Natural pyramids of ghostly form there stand like sentinels of the night, like armies prepared for battle.

In those wilds a contest, a last battle, once took place, of a kind which has occurred but a few times in the history of this country. Two bands of black-tail deer leisurely approached each other, the playful fawns racing and bounding across the matted bunch grass, thick and heavy like a great carpet, while two powerful masters approached each other as gladiators of old. On they came, the white points of their polished antlers glittering like blades of steel, stamping their feet in rage. Both were large and powerful, and as sleek as race horses. The sun was low in the Western sky and the blue haze of Indian summer hung like a fog over this grand but awful valley of death.

The bands had already mingled, but the two great masters were facing each other, with bristles erect. With heads bent down they crashed together as can only two infuriated animals. All was attention, while the brown-eyed wives stood watching their lords, who had always been so victorious in battle with other wild beasts. Crash after crash came, neither being the least baffled by the other. Each was watching for the advantage which he never gained. Every move was noted.

At the next crash, a small point was broken from an antler. With foam dropping from their mouths, their eyes green with rage, they backed off farther than ever, and with curved necks, straight as an arrow from the bow they plunged together, with a crash which resembled that of a falling tree. Their horns sprung, and they were locked in death in this wild valley, where no human eye could pity, and where no arm could aid, finally to be eaten by wolves, cougars, or bears. Perhaps the hot sun parched their tongues until they lay down in death on this, their last battlefield. We shall never know, as the only record of the battle is the deadlock horns, which were discovered and preserved and photographed by the writer.

CHAPTER XXII.

A Day Among the Clouds.

Our route lay along the foot of Cloud Peak, and as we neared a beautiful little rivulet, whose sparkling waters told of the snow far up on the mountains, we reined in our tired horses and dismounted for the night. Our packs were soon stored away, and our horses eating the luxuriant bunch grass. We made our camp on the edge of a great windfall where trees were piled together, so that no creature of any size could pass over them.

Although the sun had fallen behind the mountain, we could still see the afterglow. As I gazed at this mountain of earth, and upon the lakes and trees, I felt myself to be an infinitesimal speck in the universe. The everlasting crags of brown sandstone stood out like fortresses against the sky so blue and clear. Far up these rugged heights I could see a great bald eagle hovering over its prey. Night was fast approaching, and I had been so charmed with the glory and splendor of it all, that I forgot my partner until he sounded the supper call.

I decided to lay over and explore this wonderful mountain, as there seemed to be no end of animal life. Signs of mountain sheep, elks, bears and buffaloes were in evidence, and I was sure there were also cougars and deer. It was a wonderful country for a hunter.

Our supper was soon over and we picketed our horses

close to camp, by making a knot on our picket ropes, digging a hole about a foot deep, burying the knot and tramping the earth solid around it. We made the hole as small as possible so as not to displace much earth. We were soon in our blankets and asleep, but before long our sleep was broken by howls of timber wolves which sent a shiver through us.

Our horses were frightened beyond control, and, had we not soon lighted our fire and carefully guarded them, they would have made a supper for the wolves before dawn. These great, gaunt creatures congregated by dozens, and came into plain sight, their eyes flashing as with fire. Our great heap of pine logs and knots kept them at a reasonably safe distance until the gray began to color the east, when they sullenly and quietly slunk away to cover.

We were soon busy getting our breakfast, and while this was being prepared, we could hear the bugling of some bull elks up the mountain. Presently we started on an expedition, not so much for game as for a survey of this wonderful mountain. We rode until the ground was so steep and rocky that we were obliged to abandon our horses, and we made them fast with the picket rope. Climbing upwards, we encountered windfalls and rocks and streams. I saw several crossings where sheep had come down to the small parks of grass among the trees and slept. We alarmed many coveys of blue grouse, whose plumage was dazzling to behold. We now came to a rim of rock, and, after a hard climb, crossed it to be confronted by a beautiful lake, where hundreds of deer and elks and sheep were wont to come to slake their thirst. While we paused we could see down on the farther side, a huge cow elk and her yearling calf, drinking. Their large ears stood out to catch the sound of our feet as we approached them. We allowed them to go undisturbed, as we had no use for their flesh.

Presently we came to another lake, and here we separated. I started on a trail up the mountain, and was soon far from the lake. While resting, I was surprised to see a large silver-tip bear rushing up the trail on which I had just come. Suddenly it raised on its haunches to look below, and this was my opportunity. I leveled my rifle, took a bead on the top of its head and fired.

I shall never forget the report of the gun, nor the scream of the bear, which burst forth together. The echoes of the shot finally died away in the distance, but the roars did not cease. The ball had struck the bear just below the ear and cut an artery, and the blood spurted at every jump he gave. He went nearly to the lake, where my comrade found him dead. He was a large male and as fat as a seal. We decided to leave him where he was until we had explored the mountain top.

Our trip up the mountain was resumed and the higher we went, the colder it became. After about three hours we reached the top, and a blast of wind struck us. But we were richly paid for the ascent. It seemed as though the earth were all beneath us and that we stood like Moses of old, upon the summit of the world. All other mountains looked like mere foothills. We stood between earth and sky, overlooking a thousand valleys and winding streams. The foliage, far below, was grand beyond description and of all colors and tints. No life existed on the summit save our own, but down on the rugged sides among the lakes and springs and vegetation, thousands of elks, deer and sheep had their haunts. The wind seemed fairly to pierce our bodies, but we took the sheltered side of the mountain and descended as fast as we could.

We soon came in sight of our bear, and, to our great surprise, found another of his kind eating the one we had killed.

This was a discovery to me. I lost no time in stalking the living animal and was soon behind a tree. From this position I could see him as he tore the body to pieces. He tried to cover the remains with earth and brush, occasionally stopping to devour a portion. The sight to me was sickening beyond endurance, so I sent a ball through the monster's shoulders. He promply forgot about his dead comrade, and went down the mountain like a whirlwind, tearing and breaking everything before him. We followed him by aid of sound and blood, as fast as we could, to his lair. A great hole had been dug under a large rock, but he failed to get inside, and his great lank carcass lay stretched out just in front of it.

We commenced to skin him and I will say here, that the hunter who skins a large bear with his hide full of sand, must have a knife of very superior metal. We were forced to sharpen our knives every few moments. The toes were very hard to cut out, but after severe effort, we finally laid his skin over a pole and started for camp. We had not gone far, when we jumped a large band of black-tail deer. As we had spent our whole day in exploring, and in the killing of one bear, I took a shot at a young doe and brought it down. Its saddles were soon strung upon our pole and we trudged back to camp.

Our next encounter was with a band of mountain sheep, wending their way upward. Among them was one of the largest bucks I have ever seen, and, though I wished for his great horns, I could not possibly have carried them, so allowed the band to go unmolested. Just for sport I sent a ball near the old lord of the herd, and he turned angrily, with fight expressed in every angle of his body.

When we came out of the timber below where our horses were secured, we saw that a large band of elks had just gone through camp and had fed with them. After watering our horses and staking them for the night, we broiled our venison on a fire of quaking-asp coals. Our beds consisted of our saddle blankets, and we were soon ready for sleep. Presently the wolves began to howl in a fearful manner. My companion related several close calls he had passed through in Texas, and this narration did not tend to peaceful slumber.

When morning came we started for the Yellowstone, and, after a ride of three days, came to the old trading center at Huntley. I have never forgotten the delight of this trip and have since passed very near the same place. I still hope to revisit this locality, as I am very sure there are deposits of gold in the vicinity, for the indications all point that way. As time passes old Earth will yield up some of her very precious treasures in Wyoming and Montana, such as are yet undreamed of.

The name of the man with whom I made the expedition was supposed to be John Glenwood. I learned afterward however, that this was an assumed name, and that he had left Texas to avoid intimate connection with the hangman's rope, as he had committed murder.

CHAPTER XXIII.

A Successful Bear Hunt.

Days and months were passing away, and the many cares of life were crowding forward. The days seemed too short to accomplish the work I had set out to do. Finally I pulled up stakes and started north. When I had passed Wolf Butte, I was in the mountains, and on one high summit I stopped and took a careful survey of the surrounding country. As I gazed the old fever took me by storm. I ran my eye over the break, and was seized with an overpowering desire to penetrate its green foliage and once more feel the freedom which I had longed for so ardently of late. At length I resolved to lay over, and spend a few days in the forest. We pulled out into a green valley where wood and water were abundant and we soon had the horses cared for and our camp outfit in order.

My comrade's name was Broncho Bill—at least he was known by that name. When he had pitched the tent, he shouldered his old Sharp's and we took the trail for the haunts of big game. We had not gone far before I turned to the northwest up a small stream lined with chokecherry bushes, sagebrush and quaking asp. I had gone about two miles and the perspiration was pouring from my forehead, when I sat down on a large rock to rest. Soon I noticed that a large stone had been turned over on the opposite bank, and, on a close examination, I found unmistakable signs of

what I sought.   Holes had been dug in the ground, and
stones and logs turned over, all of which indicated the recent
visit of a bear.

In the spring a hungry bear will roll over stones and
logs that three men could not move, and then will stand up
on his hind feet and view his work, roll down the hill and
laugh like a good fellow, in the sheer joy of living.   In the
autumn he will walk up to a clump of chokecherry bushes,
stand on his haunches, encircle the branches with his front
legs, uproot the mass in one bunch, and bend them over
while he devours the fruit in great gulps.   I soon found
fresher signs, so I examined my cartridges and the lock of
my gun, and proceeded up stream with my eyes strained for
bear.   I traveled about six miles farther and came to two
large springs, where my game had wallowed in the water
and torn up the grass.

I could now see the tracks of an old bear, a two-year-old
one and a cub.   I hunted far and wide, but without success,
and, after a long, hard tramp, got back to camp empty-handed.
My comrade had killed a wolf and a wildcat during the day.
We soon had our supper and were relating our day's adventures.   A large horned owl over our heads in a cottonwood
tree, kept up his persistent "whoo, whoo," and, as I had not
fired a shot that day, I drew a bead on him and broke the
silence.   He was a very large grey fellow, and I regretted not
being able to have him stuffed.

At four in the morning we pulled out for the quaking-
asp thicket, where the night before I had abandoned the
chase. We separated and I soon sighted a large black-tailed
deer, but he disappeared in the evergreens.   I lost no time
in gaining the top of a hill where I could command a good
view of the surrounding country.   Service berries, chokecherries, currants and gooseberries were in full bloom, and

the air was fragrant with sweet odors. I was taken up with enjoyment of the place that I had almost forgotten the deer, when suddenly he emerged from a thicket and walked boldly across a little flat. He was a large buck, and had shed his horns, but the new growths were about six inches long, resembling cucumbers in shape. I was just weighing the right and wrong of shooting him, when he turned his head down the stream, gave a snort and dashed off in the direction he had come.

Rising to my feet I caught my gun, but could not command a view of the locality where he had become frightened, so I carefully crept down and took my stand where he had been. I was just arriving at the conclusion that Bill had made a sneak into my hunting ground, when I saw the tops of a bush sway to and fro as though some animal were rubbing against it. After a tedious time of waiting, the bushes moved in several places and I could scarcely hold myself, for I was certain now that I was to have a bear fight. And so it proved. At that moment a huge silver-tip bear and a cub came out into plain sight. I at once drew a bead on her head, but instantly realized that if the old one were killed first, that the cub would disappear, so I quickly decided to make sure of the young one and trust the mother to show fight, thus affording me another shot.

Before I could shoot, a third came out, and as the cub climbed around the mother, pulling and hauling, she gave it a motherly box and turned his little bearship up side down. I had waited now as long as I could for I was getting nervous. I pressed my old Bullard rifle tightly against my shoulder, drew on the two-year-old bear, and fired. The valley vibrated with the sharp crash and the ball did its fatal work. He lay quivering on his back with his feet straight up, but the report had not died away when the cub received a bullet which broke his back, as he turned toward the bushes.

I drew on the old one, but suspected that a rear shot might prove too warm for me, considering my position, as I was in a poor place for defense. The cub's cries soon hushed, and the old one returned to the bushes. I threw in a club and she caught it and crushed it to pieces.

Finally I got out of patience and fired into the place where the bushes were moving, and she roared like a mad bull, tore off down the creek, and as she went I gave her another shot in the shoulder. At this she sprang to the right and disappeared in the trees. She kept on up the hill, crashing the old limbs and twigs, so I followed and trailed her by the blood on the bushes and ground. I had crept along under the bushes for about a mile when I came almost within twenty paces of the bear, standing and looking back at me. I was almost lying down when I saw her turn half way round and realized that I was in a bad place. The bushes were low and I could not expect to escape death if I wounded her in her present position.

I felt sure she knew I was there, so I drew a quick aim at her ear and fired.

She gave one fearful bound and fell dead, tearing up the bushes and everything in her reach until her form lay quivering in the last throes of death. The whole family had been slaughtered, and, as I stood over the lifeless form of the mother, I felt a twinge of remorse. But when I saw what a fine robe she wore, I felt that I was somewhat justified, and, besides, the young cattle would now fare better in that section. It was a satisfaction to have three robes as trophies of my day's hunt.

ANTELOPE HORNS AFTER SHEDDING.

BEFORE SHEDDING,
Showing Antlers.

CHAPTER XXIV.

REGARDING THE ANTELOPE FAMILY.

Twenty years ago the Western plains were covered with antelopes (antelocapra Americana). Both in the foothills and in the valleys they were to be seen in countless numbers. The antelope is beautiful in body, pleasing in flavor, and as fleet as a race-horse. Its sides are white, its back is red. The short mane is black, as are also the stripes about the head. It has by far the keenest vision of all the animals of the plains. The horns appear just above the eyes, standing well out upon the head. They are hooked on the point with a short spur, or guard, standing at right angles with the main beam. These sharp points are used as weapons, and sometimes in battle, they become locked with the curved hooks of others of their kind, when both animals die from thirst and starvation.

The horns are annually shed, despite the statements of all the encyclopedias. This has been proven to the satisfaction of fair-minded investigators and is here shown to be a fact by an illustration of a head of an antelope killed by the author in 1877. This shedding of the outside sheath takes place in the latter part of December or early in January, leaving a velvety covering on the pith or stump. This soon becomes hard and polished and grows another bony sheath, similar to the one shed. In the fall the old horn begins to absorb at the base, and close to the head, the hair grows out through it, while the velvet or membrane commences to form under the old horn. As soon as the new membrane is formed about the pith, the outer horn falls off.

In 1877 I wrote an article about the shedding of the antelope's horns, and almost all of the old-timers declared that the specimen I had in hand was only a freak. I then began a series of examinations and was rewarded by positive proof that my original statement was correct. My second article was published in "The American Field" in 1888, which brought the entire sporting world down upon my head in contradiction. Finally, Morris Gibbs, one of America's best naturalists, came to my relief and established the fact, but there are many sportsmen who do not yet believe it.

The hair of the antelope is soft and brittle; in winter a fine wool grows underneath, which protects them from cold and storm. After the intense cold of the winter, they are the first animals to fatten on the new vegetation. The females generally have two young ones in the spring, these are spotted like deer. The antelopes have no dewclaws, or secondary hoofs, like the deer, and are easily domesticated.

Their curiosity often brings them within easy range of the hunter. They are often flagged by a red handkerchief or by a hunter lying down and keeping his feet moving around above his head. Their "woman's curiosity" has been the cause of the death of thousands of them, but not of late years, as they have learned and now avoid these tricks. Their skins, if taken in early fall and properly tanned, make very fine underclothing, and prevent one from taking cold in changeable weather.

The young antelopes leave no scent which a wolf or hound can follow. The male antelope often wanders off in summer among the pine-covered hills and lies under the shade of the trees, where it is cool, until the winter storms drive the scattering flocks together in countless thousands. In the big bend of the Yellowstone in 1877, 1878 and 1879, I have seen hundreds of thousands in one band. When they ran together, their white tails and buttocks looked like the water in a lake, when the wind is driving it into waves.

The antelope has a wonderfully keen scent, and can hear a horse's approach miles away. They sometimes detect a hunting party six or eight miles off. It takes the greatest of precaution to approach an antelope, for it is all ears and eyes and legs. They seem to fear man less than they do the wild animals. On one occasion, six antelopes which had been pursued by wolves until they were exhausted and frightened almost to death, ran before my team not more than fifty yards away for many miles, until the wolves abandoned the chase. I could easily have shot them all, but their appeal to me to save them from the sharp fangs of the wolves, in addition to the entreaty of my wife, who was with me, saved them.

There is something about a band of large gray wolves which paralyzes some animals. We once had a four-year-old horse killed and eaten by these cannibals of the plains.

Antelopes have often been fenced in by accident on the ranges, when property owners were enclosing large tracts. At the present time I know of several bands thus incarcerated. Hon. Paul McCormick, of Billings, Montana, has a band of thirty, which has increased from twelve thus confined. They have no disposition to leave the enclosure, as they are on the old range and seem to understand that they are protected; for no hunting is allowed in the park. He also has a number of elks and the two bands roam the enclosure in content.

The antelope resembles the goat family as regards the musk odor, and it is like the deer family in its symmetrical

7

body. It has no tear ducts in front of the eyes, as have the deer and elk.   The flesh is palatable, when killed at the proper time of the year, in the fall.   If the body is left intact long after death, a taint of sage is detected in the flesn, and there is also an unpleasant odor, like that of mutton not properly dressed.

Some sportsmen regard the antelope as very easy to kill. In my opinion it is the hardest of the deer family to bring to death.   I have shot an antelope nine times, driving that number of 45-70-450 bullets through its body, and then it traveled ten miles before it fell.   Sometimes I have shot them lengthwise through the body, but seldom have I seen them fall where they were shot.

CHAPTER XXV.

GOOD SPORT IN PATOHAR BASIN.

The month of September, 1882, was of unusual beauty and charm to the hunter in the region of the Yellowstone River. Foliage of gorgeous reds and golds and browns was scattered over the thousand hills. Myriads of grouse roamed about, feasting on the delicious harvest of berries. The jack snipe busily plied his long bill in the marsh, searching for insects, and the jay and red squirrel battled vociferously for pine nuts.

A jollier set of sportsmen then we never graced a camp-fire. The party consisted of Mr. Shields, of "The American Field," of Chicago; Mr. R. J. Sawyer, of Menominee, Michigan, who is as keen a sportsman as ever shouldered a rifle; Mr. Wise, of Michigan, who flourished a 45-75 Winchester, and, from his use of this weapon, convinced us he "had been there before;" Mr. Huffman, a photographer from Miles City; Uncle Ed. Forest, an old-timer, who had played "hide-and-seek" with the Sioux nation for the last thirty years; my son Willie, and myself.

The mountains were alive with animals, and each member of our party was eager to try his skill with the rifle. We pressed along the beautiful valley of Clark's Fork, and white-tailed deer were seen in the distance, skirting the banks of the river. As our caravan moved along, a coyote broke cover from a clump of sagebrush, and, with his tail waving in the breeze, glided like a shadow across the valley. As he rushed on, bullets followed, sometimes covering him with sand. His zigzag course resembled lightning, but he soon left us far behind.

The white sides of a large number of antelopes, quietly feeding on the rich grasses, attracted us presently, and, after a stalk of some miles, we came upon them. By a careful maneuver we succeeded in nearly surrounding them, and soon a volley was poured into them from three sides. Two of their number fell to the ground. The others started in a circle and our bullets cut the earth all about them. They seemed bewildered, without realization of the approaching danger. A large buck antelope with his head erect, bounded high, his sleek glossy sides looking like silver. But death was on his trail, for simultaneously with the report of my rifle, he tumbled forward. The other boys secured five in all. There was much excitement and waste of material, but the amateur must learn to aim ahead of the fleet antelope if he wishes to hit the mark.

We planned a great raid on the trout of Bennett Creek, turned out part of the channel and made a lake far down the valley, which is still in good order, and is still a paradise for the finny tribe. A day was spent here in resting and feasting, during which time we killed two more antelopes. After taking a photograph of the camp we proceeded up the little stream known as Patohar, and after considerable meandering, camped above the place of the Chapman brothers. Here we prepared to hunt for bears and elks.

After the regular camp building, erecting tents, making beds of fragrant pine boughs and preparing fire pits, we were ready for the morning, which always comes soon to the tired hunter. The next day was spent in inspecting the country and noting game trails. We all came in rather disappointed,

BUCK ANTELOPE.

Showing Horns in Full Growth.

as we had found no fresh signs, excepting Uncle Ed., who claimed he had seen nine elks at a great distance on the mountain. I now came to the conclusion that the game was higher up and resolved to hunt there the next day.

In the morning we started in different directions and were soon lost to each other's sight. After a dreary climb, I rested on a crag and cast a parting look at our camp, nestling in the chokecherry trees by the creek. I noticed the relative positions of Heart Mountain and several other landmarks, and then proceeded on my way. Higher and higher I wandered up the mountain, where the pine cones and the bunch grass formed a carpet of extreme softness. Finally I started round the mountain and decided to cross a gulch, where I could see in the distance some quaking asps growing, for I knew there must be water in the vicinty.

I had not proceeded far when I was delighted to hear a stick snap. I sat down and waited until I was tired and out of patience, but at length, indistinctly, I saw something move, far below be. It proved to be a white-tail doe creeping along, and I could soon see her glossy side near the water. Her great brown eyes glistened like diamonds, her ears moved back and forth as she advanced gracefully and noiselessly, scanning every object. Instinctively I could feel my arm raising slowly and my old Bullard coming into a line with the beautiful neck. In a moment a leaden messenger crashed through the sleek neck and this queen of the hills was lying bathed in blood.

As I pulled her out of the dense wood I heard some of our boys coming down the canyon. They stopped and in a short time we had the deer on a horse and had started toward camp. We were ravenously hungry and soon had a fine repast, consisting of fresh venison, potatoes, canned pears, dried fruit, boiled onions and coffee.

After dinner I started up the left fork of the Patohar, and after climbing a bald hill, sat down to view the hills and valleys. My boy, Willie, accompanied me on his pony and presently he detected something down the mountain. I turned and saw a young grizzly, bounding down the other side of the mountain. In an instant I was on my feet, and, after giving careful directions to my son, went after his bearship. I watched him carefully until he began to feed in a berry patch, and then I went as fast as I could run toward that place. I was tired when I had located him, almost out of breath, but, having taken a short rest, I concluded to give him a surprise.

After a careful survey of the ground, I decided that my position was disadvantageous, and that the bear was going from me over a divide. Instant action was imperative. I concluded that I would break his shoulder, and, by the time he could get to me, one hundred yards distant, I would have him pretty well filled with lead. After throwing in a death-seed, I took deliberate aim at his shoulderblade and fired. The bear was more than surprised, and, with a roar which sounded as if the infernal regions had been stormed, he was almost on top of me before the smoke cleared away.

I gave him another shot at about ten paces and jumped to one side. He dashed at the smoke and his roars almost deafened me. Quick as thought I threw in another shell, sprang across a little rill, and, as I landed, I heard him coming. I drew another hasty aim and fired. The fire and powder burnt his face severely and the ball struck him just under the eye, tearing his entire brain to pieces. Just then I heard something snort behind me, and wheeled around to see my boy within twenty paces of me. The little pony was snorting like an antelope at the bear, which lay in a pool of blood.

The first shot had broken his shoulder, the second had struck him in the breast and gone through his lungs, the third had broken his skull. Any of the shots would have killed him, but not until after he could have killed half-a-dozen men. He weighed about five hundred pounds, and was as vicious an animal as I ever saw, fighting until the last spark of life had fled. I soon had his skin off, and found his head and shoulders were a mass of blood and broken bones.

This day revealed the whereabouts of considerable game, and Mr. Huffman had flushed a large band of elks of all ages. They were three separate bands, and he had exhausted his supply of cartridges at seventy-five to a hundred yards distance, but had no elk to show, although he had wounded several. We put in two days in hunting this band, which had gone to the southwest. The yard where they camped showed that there were nearly one hundred and fifty of them roaming around. As the rutting season had commenced, they were splitting up. The bulls were herding the cows in all directions, and I knew it would be no use to follow them, but would be better to hunt a new band.

We were getting desperate now, for our supply of meat was getting low, so we set out up the north mountain side. After a hard climb we reached the quaking-asps and springs of water. We paired off and had not gone far when we heard the elk tearing through the bushes, and soon Shield's rifle rang out three times in quick succession. All was now confusion. Shield had killed a cow and wounded a young bull. Sawyer and I had came close together, and I could hear some animal going in his direction, when his old 50 Winchester belched its compliments with an explosive bang. I soon reached him, but the fog was so dense that I could see nothing, but presently we found a large cow elk, with one of her hind legs almost torn from her body.

We all returned to camp thoroughly soaked. After supper Shields supplied himself with matches, an oilcloth coat and his rifle, and went to watch his elk, which we had left in a tree. This was a good idea, for the bears were thick. In the morning we could hear a cannonading which sounded like a skirmish, and I think Shields and a bull elk must have got buffaloed, as there were fully twelve shots fired. However, he secured a fine bull with a beautiful pair of antlers, though one was shot almost off in the fray. After the game was all dressed we started up the mountain with horses, after the old bull and Sawyer's cow elk.

We were hard at work skinning the bull, when three bears charged us like Comanche Indians. They came with roars and growling, snapping their teeth like steel traps. They advanced until they were within a few paces, when the uproar in camp caused them to stop and look. Horses were plunging, snorting and bucking. Our rifles cracked and increased the din. The old bear and one of the younger ones were killed, one making his ecape.

We now had a fine bait to watch, and the bears literally tore up the earth around us every night. Sawyer got a shot at a large grizzly, but missed. Wise also missed one, but, as he had killed two before, we were well supplied with bear meat.

I went up one evening and took up a station to watch the carcasses. The grouse were thick and were flying all around. I had almost concluded to get some of them for supper when I heard the rushing footsteps of a bear. I sat behind a large pine, and, as my bear came into view, I sent a 45 bullet through his neck, cutting his jugular vein and breaking his neck and back.

Our happiness was now about complete, for we had all killed a large amount of game, and Mr. Sawyer had tried his new gun on elks, bears and antelopes and found its killing qualities all that he could wish. Mr. Wise had found his old

45 sufficient for bears. Mr. Shields had killed his boss elk, Uncle Ed. had hammered the game all around. So we broke camp after five weeks of unbounded pleasure in the Patohar basin.

After traveling seventy-five miles over the Clark's Fork valley, we landed in Billings, all brown with sun and wind, as stout and hearty a set of fellows as ever returned from a hunting trip. From here each went his way, but it will be a long time before the events of that hunt will be forgotten by the participants.

CHAPTER XXVI.

THE SPORTSMEN'S OLD HAUNTS—Indian summer—on the mountain—a big horn chase—my largest ram.

In 1886 I was in Cooke City, where my dental work had called me. It was four years since I had indulged myself in a regular hunt. I had arranged for a hunting trip with some friends, and the appointed hour had passed and they had not appeared. My old Bullard stood in the corner. Cartridges, belt, knife and hunting suit, all were ready, and I felt the keenest disappointment.

Many changes had taken place in the sportsmen's old haunts. Where game had recently roamed the forests was now taken as ranges for domestic stock. The game had been driven far back into the high crags and mountains, such as the Index and Electric peaks, which stand eleven and twelve thousand feet above the level of the sea, the hunter being forced to climb those rugged cliffs to find satisfactory game.

The following morning even brought no news of my comrades. Anxiety and suspense overcame me. I grasped my faithful old friend, threw down the lever and surveyed the inside which gleamed like a mirror. It was my Bullard rifle, 45 calibre, eighty-five grains of powder, ten pounds weight and ten shots. I seized my cartridge belt, my knife, a cold lunch and started out.

The sun shone warmly and the smoke from the smelters gave an appearance of Indian summer. I soon gained a forest of pines whose boughs were loaded with nuts. The little red squirrels were merrily cutting the burrs and chattering among the branches. The mountain jay clamored in the tops of the trees where the nuts were thickest. The little chipmunk was gathering up what fell to the earth, busily depositing it in his winter home. All living creatures were active. How natural it all seemed!

I crossed Soda Butte Creek and started up the mountain. Fallen timber, cordwood and old tree-tops almost blocked the way, but I pressed on higher and higher up the grand old mountain until I was almost out of breath. Towering up in the clouds stood Index and Pilot peaks covered with evergreens and snow. I often was forced to stop to catch my breath in this high altitude. Looking far down into the depths I could see the little stream glistening in the sunlight. Cooke City looked like a group of toy houses. Once more I turned my eyes toward the summit. Its grandeur and sublimity were almost overpowering.

Surely such a place must be the home of the bighorn sheep. I scanned one shelf after another and swept my eyes along until on a sharp projecting cliff I beheld some living thing. The old-time thrill went through my frame like a shock of electricity. Before I could make out what the object was, I hastened along over rocks, bushes, scrub junipers and beds of green moss. Finally I could see the grayish outlines of what appeared to be a bighorn. By taking a circuitous route I gained an easy distance and good range. After a long hard climb I found myself on a high peak, destitute of life, for my bighorn had disappeared around the peak.

At length I landed on his feeding ground and soon found his tracks in the loose dirt. His hoof marks were like those of a yearling steer. I set out upon his trail, keeping low behind the rocks. After traveling about a mile he had started to run, so I gave up the hopes of ever again seeing him and started up the mountain. After going across the country for some time, I flung myself down upon a moss patch, completely tired out. I looked down upon a world of mountains. Bear Tooth stood about seven miles away. The Stinking Water, Clark's Fork, Cradle Creek, the Hoodoos and the Tetons could all be located with accuracy.

While I was locating different portions of the country I perceived an animal on a little mound about four hundred yards to my right. It was feeding and I could see only its back. It would not be possible to go closer, for I would be in plain view all of the way. Presently it turned, walked leisurely to the top of the mound, broadside to me and stopped.

What a sight for these latter days! There stood my bighorn. The sky was the background and his erect head, his large round body and well-set limbs made a striking picture. I raised my globe sight to four hundred yards, threw in a cartridge, and, drawing the butt closer to my shoulder, pressed the trigger. A stream of fire, a deafening report, and the echoes rumbled down, down, until all was again quiet. The ram had made one bound and was out of sight. I threw in another cartridge and with all of my speed ran to the spot.

There was visible a tuft of hair and a spattering of blood. About one hundred yards below he lay dead. He was the largest ram I had ever seen and his large horns were half buried in the sand. His mouth was still full of herbs, his sleek coat of blue hair was like the down of thistles. He weighed about three hundred pounds, and his head was all that I could carry. I dressed him nicely, took his pelt and started to return. After hours of fatigue I reached home, and dressed his lordship's head, which now, with other specimens which have fallen to the music of my old Bullard, adorns my home.

Later I returned for the carcass, and, after getting his

BIG HORN RAM.

Photo from Life.

saddle off, my pony looked like an old workhorse from the great exertion of the trip.   I often think in these latter days of that wild ride through the mountains and sigh for another such September day, and for my old hunting-horse, which would lie down and keep still at a moment's warning.

CHAPTER XXVII.

Goat Hunting at Dearborn Canyon.

With my traveling outfit of dental instruments and my rifle, I alighted from the overland coach at Sun River Crossing, Montana, determined to enjoy a few days in hunting before settling down to work. I found a half-breed Frenchman who was just about to start for Augusta, a little town on the south fork of Sun River. As I wished to lose no time, I asked him if he would take me and my outfit to Augusta.

"How much you give?" was his answer.

"What do you want?"

He replied that he would like to have a little tea. I bought him a pound of black tea for fifty cents, and a delighted expression came into his face when I handed him the coveted article. We soon entered his spring wagon and started. He was very inquisitive as to my plans and work. I told him I was a dentist going to Augusta, and from there into the mountains after goats.

"Mountain goat?"

"Yes," said I, "I want to find some goats. Where do you live?"

"Dearborn canyon. Heaps of goats high up there now."

We rattled along and he told me all about the game in his locality. Before we reached our destination he informed me that his horses would take me after goats if I so desired. We arrived in Augusta about dark, and stopped there over night. Early next morning with ample provisions, we set out for the half-breed's home. Our course lay through Hay basin, a lonely little valley about a mile wide. The country was dotted with small lakes and almost covered with ducks.

We reached my guide's home, if it could be called a home, about noon. His possessions were a little log cabin, four lank cayuses, a dog and half-a-dozen children. There seemed to be a family resmblance between the animals and children. His wife owned most of the flesh on the premises, her weight being two hundred and fifty pounds. I had taken the precaution to bring a good bed with me, so was assured of cleanliness and comfort. After examining all of our outfit the curiosity of the children was satisfied. I began to clean my gun and prepare for the morning.

As only one bed was visible, I wondered how this family of eight would manage to sleep. Presently a large tick was taken from the bed and spread upon the floor. The children were all stored away in the bed and not a word was said, but several pairs of roguish black eyes peered out under the covers while I arranged my blankets near by. The parents then filled their pipes and began to smoke.

In their plain cabin, with just enough to keep soul and body together, the happiness of these people seemed complete. The half-breed had married a Flathead squaw, and, during the time of Reil's rebellion had moved to Montana where he has lived and roamed ever since. After relating many buffalo and other frontier stories, we turned in for the night. We arose late in the morning, but were not long in getting off, as our pack horses were in the stable and our provisons were soon packed.

We began to ascend Dearborn canyon on the north wall. Each of us rode one horse and Lafarge, the half-breed, led the pack horse. While going over some rough ground, the pack horse contrived to get his lariat under the tail of the horse ridden by Lafarge. The bronco bucked furiously, Lafarge meanwhile yelling lustily. Finally the animal lay down and rolled over, unseating Lafarge. It was fun for me, and I laughed until I was sore.

Making another start, we reached the first park, which was a splendid place for deer, but not high enough for goats. We continued our way beyond the park, and began the ascent of the main range of the mountains. After three hours of hard climbing and pulling, we reached the golden summit.

Here was a grand sight. We could see the valley for miles below, the beautiful winding Sun River and its tributaries. October in her multi-colored splendor had already dyed the forest leaves. We made camp, secured our horses and started to survey the summit. As we strolled along thousands of feet below us we could see where the goats had cut deep trails among the soft rocks, and near us were plenty of signs of recent visitation.

We found a spring and plenty of wood at the head of a canyon, and made our camp at this point. Goats had been there within twenty-four hours. We rested well, disturbed only by the mourning of the wind among the trees during the night.

After breakfast we picketed our horses, and, filling our belts with cartridges, started for a rugged cliff about a mile away, which was partly covered with evergreens. Cougar signs were visible in the sand and this was a good indication, as the cougar or mountain lion is always to be found in the vicinity of other game. We toiled on and upward until we reached a beautiful open spot, which ran parallel with the mountains.

While we sat viewing the beauties of this grand park, we saw a band of black-tail deer feeding off toward a canyon on the north side.   There were five in the band, and they soon disappeared down the canyon, about three hundred yards away.   Lafarge wanted to pursue them, but I was after goats, for I could kill deer anywhere.   So I told him we would not try to molest the deer until after we had killed some goats. We turned to the south and passed down a series of what might be called stone steps, until we landed on a narrow shelf covered with a fine moss and a few scrub pines.

Here we found fresh sheep and goat signs.   The animals had gone around to the west side of the mountain, toward which we followed as fast as the condition of the ground would permit.   After a long walk, we rounded a heavy boulder which had fallen from the ledge above, and there surprised five goats that were carelessly sauntering about, picking up the finest moss.   They saw us and started to run.   I shot at the leader and killed him in his tracks.   A second shot killed another just as they disappeared around a curve.   We followed at our utmost speed but we never again saw the remaining three, nor could we find where they went.

The dead goats were splendid specimens, whose sleek black horns looked like polished ebony.   As they were very heavy we skinned them, and only took their skins and the hind quarters, but these made a heavy load for us to carry out of this mountain defile.   After great exertion, we ascended our stone steps and rested on the mountain top.

I felt now that my hunt was over, but Lafarge wanted some deer meat.   To please him we went after the black-tail deer we had seen in the morning.   I was sure they would not go far, and while he went after our pack horses, I followed the deer.   They had passed ovr the brow of the hill, where, after a close inspection, I found them lying among the rocks. They saw us, ran toward the goat trail, and as they flew past me I shot three in rapid succession, letting the two old ones go unmolested. We dressed them and packed the choicest parts to our camp, where we had a royal feast on venison marrow-bones and liver. We had hunted all day and were as hungry as mountaineers only can be.

We arose early on the next morning, packed our goats and deer, alternately leading and riding our horses down the trail toward home. I never before saw such a happy squaw and youngsters as received us on our return. We unloaded the venison, which, with our provisions, was stowed away in the cabin.

After supper, from miles around, young half-breeds came in, and I was treated to the sight of a dance which was unique in the amount of alcohol consumed, and the quantity and quality of music evoked from the violin.

As I was to return to Augusta the following day, I took my bed outside the cabin and went to sleep. About eleven the next morning we set out for Augusta, and found that another dance was announced there for that night. From this trip I brought only one deer and the hides and horns of the two goats back with me, but pleasant recollections will always be associated with its remembrance.

CHAPTER XXVIII.

After Elk on Ten Sleep River.

In 1890, some time after I had abandoned hunting as a profession, I was in Buffalo, Wyoming, where I had established a dental office. One morning Cal Jennings, one of the finest big game hunters of Wyoming, was brought into my office by Mr. Chappell, and nothing would do but we must all join in an old-fashioned elk hunt. I gave the subject due deliberation and concluded to join them in a quest of the old monarch of the mountains; for it had been a long time since I had seen him at large.

Mr. Jennings declared he knew just where a band was to be found, so we talked the matter over, and set the time of our departure three days later. We secured a good outfit, and I finished up my work preparatory to leaving. As the day approached I began to feel the old fever. We were all busy in packing our provisions and camp fittings, but Mr. Jennings had not yet made his appearance, and we were wondering what delayed him.

Just at this moment we heard a rattling, and, looking up the road, we saw four fine animals hitched to a light wagon, in which sat Jennings, his long whip sounding like firecrackers.

Dashing up, he made a circle after the custom of an overland coach driver, and stopped to take aboard our groceries and bedding. Our effects were piled into the wagon in a few minutes and one crack of his whip sent the horses away like a flash. Through the kindness of Mr. Chaplin, a wealthy farmer and cattlegrower, I was loaned a fine saddle pony. Chappell rode Dr. Watkins' iron-gray steeple-chaser; Mr. Dickey rode his own fleet mare, and Mr. Jennings also took along his old reliable pony, which was ridden by Mr. Erwin Whitcomb, who completed the party. My friend, Chappell, and myself remained to bring up the rear on horseback.

Our horses were in good condition and traveled well. When we ascended the top of the hill, we could see our team and horsemen wending their way far in the distance. We were now about five miles from the base of the mountain, so we pressed forward. Having ascended a gulch a long distance, we finally came to what I supposed was the road which went up perpendicularly, but, on nearing the spot, it was found to be a pole chute. We turned to the left and found our teamster, Cal, toiling up the narrow way. Here we were fortunate enough to find a man hauling lumber who gave us the aid of one of his teams. After a pull of more than an hour, we succeeded in getting up the worst portion of the mountain.

Presently we came to a halt and camped for dinner at an old sawmill. Our horses were soon eating. Each member of our company tried to outdo the others in the preparation of dinner, and, in a few minutes, all were appeasing mountain appetites. After dinner our route lay over a beautiful prairie with stretches of pine timber. The warm sun brought out the red squirrels, and the ever busy "camp robber" was chattering, as he plied his ivory bill to the pine cone, devouring the nuts. We made a long drive over rough roads and struck our camp on the north fork of Powder River, where Cal had planned that we would spend the night. Chappell and I stole a march on the others, got in first, located camp, picketed our horses, and set out after the festive black-tails.

We headed for a rimrock fringed with pine, dotted with quaking-asps and box elders, and made a drive hunt. Chappell took the right and I the left, agreeing to meet at a certain point of rocks. I had just crossed the little stream when Chappell's old Bullard rifle awoke the neighborhood with a piercing sound. I hastily threw a cartridge into the chamber of my gun and strained my eyes for deer, but none came in sight. I was now on my mettle and resolved that if there was a deer in that country I would add him to our larder, so I plunged into the quaking-asp, from there went on to the pines and the rimrock, but a few old buck tracks were all I could find.

It was dark when I turned to go to camp and I heard, although very faintly, in the distance the snap of a stick, but my practiced ear rarely errs in such a matter. I marked the direction, crept carefully along and listened. I could hear the leaves pack under the tread as the footsteps came closer, and I believed that I had stalked a lion, so I lay down in the trail to surprise his majesty when he came up to me. In a moment I could see something approaching very cautiously, and drew my rifle to my face and raised the hammer, but held my thumb carefully on it. On the figure came and I was sure that I had game, but, as I never shot at random in my life, this was a time for me to be on my guard. Another stick cracked, and then I began to think it was nothing worth my while and lowered my gun. Presently I could see a black object, which anyone would have sworn was a bear, crawling under some fallen brush only about forty yards away.

I said in a low tone, "Is that you, Chappell?"

The answer came, "You bet, what are you doing away up here? I thought you had gone to camp."

"One careless shot and you would have been an angel," I replied.

"I don't hunt with them kind of fellows."

We had a good laugh over the surprise. Chappell had failed to bring down his deer, so that put an end to my hopes of fresh meat for supper. We were now two or three miles from camp and had come directly together in the heart of the forest, a mile from where we agreed to meet. "Never shoot at any game until you can see it wink," was a lesson I was thoroughly taught when a boy, and I should have surely killed my companion if I had fired contrary to this rule.

When we reached camp supper was ready, and we did it ample justice. In the evening we listened as Cal told where to find the alleged band of bulls, then the exact location of the cows and calves and also of the rimrock, where deer were in number "like flies at a meat market." But I had hunted the mountains in palmier days than these, and knew that game would be hard to find in such fine weather. The pleasant campfire and our warm beds were just the thing for us that night.

After a refreshing sleep and a warm breakfast, we continued our march, having about the same luck as the day before, except that Chappell tried ti extract a shell from his rifle and broke the shell extractor. He said this would surely hoodoo him for the trip. Presently when we came to some thick pine trees I saw a grouse, dismounted and fired a shot at it. The feathers flew from its body in a great cloud, and I thought I had torn a whole wing off, but, as no one of our party saw the bird fly, and it could not be found in the tree where I had located it, we came to the conclusion that it had dematerialised.

Our journey now became more interesting. The scenery was wilder. Civilization was farther behind us. After going a few miles we found some elk signs and here Chappell and I took a turn through the mountains. We saw that the

elk had made a straight line for our evening camp, so we
bore further westward, where we found plenty of fresh deer
signs. As we were climbing a steep bank above a deep creek,
having our guns carelessly dangling in the slings, through
some quaking-asps I saw the outlines of a black-tail deer. I
jumped from my pony and in a moment had the old Bullard
ready for business. As I crawled up a little, I discovered
five other deer in different places, but could see none of them
plainly. But there was no chance to get a better shot, so I
drew a bead on the one standing nearest me and fired.

The instant the gun cracked there was a scampering
through the burnt timber, and they were gone. I fired two
more shots after them, but without effect. I began to think
that we were, as Chappell had said, "hoodooed," or that the
deer were bewitched. I went to where my mark had been
standing and found that my ball had struck two bushes, the
first being torn almost off. I discovered pieces of deer hair
but no blood. I never had made such a shot in my life before, for the deer had stood broadside, not over seventy-five
feet away, and it was a clear miss.

While we were talking the matter over, a large buck
came to the edge of the opening, not a hundred yards below
us. He stood out in perfect outline with his head erect, his
massive antlers gleaming in the last rays of the setting sun.
His large eyes were like coals of fire, his hair was on end,
for it was the rutting season. I could see that a small tree
was directly in our line of sight, but one step would clear
away this trouble, and, as I moved to one side, raising my
gun, the buck jumped behind a tree and was gone. I ran
after him, hoping to get one shot, but he had disappeared, and
I at last surely began to think I was doomed to disappointment for the entire trip. These two sore disappointments
were so close together that I called them twins.

We ranged the pine hills far and wide, and finally found ourselves on the top of a mountain. Twilight was setting in, but we were determined to have some meat, if meat was to be had, so we kept on until it was dark, when we found to our dismay that we were on the rimrock. Everything soon became the same color, so we dismounted and led our horses, plodding along in darkness. We tried to descend at a dozen places, each one proving worse than the last, and it must have been at least nine o'clock when we succeeded in getting down over the rocks and dead trees. As our camp was below us on the creek, another hour was spent getting to it, and we again took supper without fresh meat. That five men, hunters, should be out in the wilds for two days and kill nothing was a disgrace to the party.

The next day's march was to carry us into the heart of our hunting ground to our main camp. We held a council, and Chappell and Jennings, who knew the ground, agreed on the location of the camp. Chappell and myself then started across the country, eager to get some game, as we now began to feel the need of fresh meat. The afternoon was spent in quest of black-tail deer. Creek beds, southern hillsides, mountain tops, rimrocks and the pine forests afforded us no opportunity to shoot, and when our party reassembled at the night camp on Ten Sleep, we were all empty-handed. The mountains surrounded us on the north, east and west, and the three forks of the Ten Sleep River were alive with trout. Signs of deer and elk had been seen, and we were all sure that the morrow would find our camp well supplied with meat, and meat in abundance.

While we sat eating our supper of canned food, hot biscuits and coffee under the towering pines, Cal told us that our supper the next night would consist principally of elk steak. Chappell declared he was going to have a deer's rib roasted, while Dicky said he "was too high-toned for such common grub, and would provide some mountain grouse." A school of trout, which Whitcomb claimed to have captured, he informed us would be fried for supper. We had placed our tent just at the edge of the heavy timber, so that the game could not see it, and our mess wagon was completely hidden from view. A clear cold spring was near by, where the elk came to drink. Grass was plenty, wood abundant, and we were now in a real hunter's paradise. At a short distance, the clear waters of the Ten Sleep River were dashed into foam and countless thousands of speckled trout were to be seen.

The evening was spent in preparation for the great to-morrow, when our camp was to be filled with elk, deer and the fat of the land. We arose with the morning sun still behind the eastern mountain. Breakfast was soon over, and we got ready for the chase. Before we separated, four of us agreed to meet at a designated mountain spur in the evening. We hunted without adventure the whole day, and when night came, assembled around the supper table with a cover of grouse as the best showing of the day. Of course, we all knew where the elk had gone, and were going to take them in the next day. After supper we joined in a great plot to do the elk of that vicinity bodily injury. The boys had piled up a rick of pitch pine, the flames shot up almost as high as the trees, and the moon and stars shone out until it seemed almost like day. All at once there was a flash of light and a meteor shot across the heavens, leaving a track of fire behind it.

After our hard day's hunt we lost no time in sleeplessness, and the cry of the owl awoke us early in the morning. Chappell and Dickey took their course to the north, while Cal Jennings and I peretrated Ten Sleep canyon, which we found an ideal home for game. However, we sighted none, and climbed the mountain toward the south. Finally we came to the divide, where we dismounted and looked over the country. As we were remounting, Cal caught sight of a moving object. After a careful scrutiny we discovered several others, and, as Cal knew there were no cattle in that country, we felt sure that our long time of hunting was now to be rewarded. We led our horses down the mountain, and commenced stalking in earnest, for we could see fresh signs, which made us more confident that our chances for fresh meat were good.

When we reached the creek, we watered our horses, drank of the cold stream, and found that the water reeds had recently been eaten close to the earth. Elk signs were abundant and the band had gone directly toward our place of discovery on the mountain. We mounted and started on the run around a foothill, which seemed to be a good point of observation. We dismounted, tied the bridle reins to our ponies front feet, and prepared to move on the unsuspecting game. As we crept over the ground, I filled the old Bullard to overflowing with cartridges, for I was well aware that I was with one of the finest game shots in Wyoming, and was resolved to give him an exhibition of my skill at the first opportunity. At that moment I saw the back of some gray object moving slowly to our left, and could easily have driven a ball through it. Instead of firing, I called Cal's attention to it. Just as he turned to look the old steer raised his head, gave one snort anrd started away down the mountain side, accompanied by the whole drove.

I was sorely tempted to shoot after them, for we were getting desperate, and Cal threw down his old white hat in profound disgust. We swore vengeance on the next living object, should it be cattle or game, and with this vow set out for camp. After a long, weary ride, groping through dark woods, we reached there at nine o'clock, having killed two blue grouse on our way. Our tired horses were put to feed and we commenced to get supper. Of course, all of the members of the company had seen fresh signs of game. From eight to ten square miles of country had been hunted faithfully without success. This was certainly discouraging, for the snow was likely to fall any day and shut us in for the winter. After supper I got sixteen tail-feathers out of the grouse, put them in my hatband, and "made medicine" for the next day's luck. The boys all took some of the feathers, and we turned in for the night, tired out and sleepy.

Early in the morning Cal and I started out together, and I now proposed to take the second rimrock. I had noticed, when crossing a high divide on the last trip we made, several fresh signs of black-tail deer. We started for a high range of hills between the east and west forks of Ten Sleep. We traveled until our horses were tired, and the higher up we went, the more signs we saw. After a hard effort we gained an eminence whence we could survey the country.

While taking observations, I saw several objects about six miles to the west, on the other side of the canyon, but, as we had no glass, we concluded not to go after them, for our experience of the day before was too fresh in our minds to favor such chances. We started down a slope which led us to the main canyon, and came to where five deer had just passed down. After dismounting and tieing our horses, we set out on the trail, which went directly toward the canyon. The deer had been feeding leisurely along, cropping the rich bunch grass.

"If I believed in witchcraft at all," said Cal, "I should believe that the bad spirit had taken possession of me this trip, and you know Chappell is certain that he is bewitched for the trip ever since he broke his ejector at Powder River."

Cal, who was just then above me, saw a large doe that was out of my sight, and raised his rifle. The clear stinging report woke the hills, the echoes sounding and resounding for miles below. We hurried to the spot, a hundred yards away, and found he had scored a clean miss. It was one of those unaccountable and unexplainable misses, which, at times, fall to the lot of all hunters. The deer had bounded down the chasm, headlong, tearing rocks and dirt in their flight as they sprang like mountain sheep until they reached the depths below. We remounted, started for another rim-rock and were slowly climbing the south side of the hill, when we found another trail where five more deer had gone up. We thought this was our last chance.

We were now close to a grove of jack-pine trees, and as Cal came near the edge, I saw him begin to pull at his Winchester and tumble off his pony. I jumped from my horse, gun in hand, and started for Cal, who had already fired twice. As these shots were fired through bushes, he missed his game, and, though both horses started to run, we did not heed them. Nothing could divert us from deer. I now gained a good inside view of the grove, the trees being low and far apart.

One doe was running straight up the hill and I threw my gun to my shoulder and fired. She stood still and I knew she was hit. Four more deer started at right angles down the hill, and a young buck received a broadsider, which landed him quickly. During all of this time the one I had shot first had not moved, so Cal raised his Winchester and shot her through the neck, which finished her. We soon had her cleaned and secured upon Cal's horse behind the saddle, he supposing this was all the game we had. I started for the other doe and found it, much to Cal's delight and surprise. We cleaned this one, tied it on my horse and then I went to the place where the buck had disappeared. This animal was soon found, and Cal was speechless with gratification at the turn in our fortune.

He insisted that the other one had gotten away down the rimrock, but I was confident that I had brought him also to earth. As it was dark, and our horses were heavily loaded, we concluded to wait until morning before we searched for him. After two hours of hard travel over logs and through bushes and trees, we could see the bright campfire blazing up among the tall pines, and a thrill of joy crept over us as we neared its warmth. We closely surveyed the camp from a distance, to see if any game adorned it. None was in sight, so we rode proudly in to receive the congratulations of our comrades and started our first venison cooking of this trip. Soon the gentle zephyr was scented with the aroma of the juicy meat, and we all had a splendid supper of liver, steak, hot biscuits, fried onions and roasted potatoes, with an abundance of good coffee.

We cut away some limbs and hung our deer as high as we could reach, but their heads and shoulders rested on the ground. Cal said that we would get all the game we wanted now as we had a start. We all retired late to rest, but were up early to go after the other deer and to look for the others we expected to kill. In the old snow we found bear tracks, and those of a mountain lion also, but, as the snow was almost gone, we could not track them far, and were compelled to leave this game until another snow should fall. When we reached the scene of the encounter of the night previous, a myriad of magpies were devouring our deer. We went to the one we killed the night before, found the birds were eating its insides, so we cut some pine boughs and filled the deer's body with them to prevent the birds from getting into it.

I now started to look for some signs of my other deer.

I went first and found the place I had seen him give the last bound. Blood was in his trail and on both sides. I followed and about fifty yards beyond found a fine young buck, lying in the top of an old pine. I took out my knife, opened him and found him perfectly fresh. We packed the two deer on the pony and started. Whitcomb and Dick returned to camp, while the remainder of our party, started out after elks. We put in a hard afternoon on the elk trail, following it for miles, without finding them. Returning to camp at last, tired and hungry, we resolved to try another part of country on the next day. In order to change our luck, we made medicine that evening. I think all of us were adorned with feathers.

Early in the morning, before the sun was up, Cal set out to look for the horses, but soon came down the hill like a race horse, saying there were thirty-five elks in the park. The expression on his face was serious, so each of us darted for his gun, cartridge belt and knife. Some of us were only partially dressed, but we lost no time in answering the summons. We were soon where the elk had crossed. In the white and crisp morning's frost were tracks of cows and calves. A large bull had brought up the rear and the trail led toward the large body of timber which was miles in width. After following to this point we held a council. It was decided that Cal and I were to make a circle to the north, and if we came on the band, we were to wait for the others.

When we had gone a mile we came to the south end of a park, where the whole band had turned and started northward, and, to our surprise, we found no hunters in pursuit. After a close survey, we could see that the band was heading toward Ten Sleep lake, far above timber line. The other boys had gone to get breakfast, but Cal and I decided not to eat until we partook of elk steak.

We started over dead timber, windfalls, and rocks, slipping and sliding along until we came to where the mountain suddenly gave way to the valley below. Amost formidable hill raised prominently on the other side, and the trail was so difficult that sometimes we were scarcely able to follow it at all. At last we came to an opening in the timber, and I told Cal I would make a small circuit, with the understanding that neither of us was to shoot till the other appeared.

I had reached a point from whence I could see the other mountain side covered with burnt timber, and was watching closely for elk, when Cal's rifle broke the stillness. I looked in his direction and could see one black-tail struggling in death's embrace and another thundering down through the burnt timber. I quickly threw my Bullard to my face and fired, breaking the deer's neck. When we had the two elks dressed and hung up, we saw that the others had taken flight at the shot and had darted back on their tracks. This gave us a straight run of ten miles and on our way we often found where they had rested on the north hillside in the snow. The day was warm, and we pressed them as fast as we could until we came to the east fork of Ten Sleep. Here they wandered around and made several attempts to cross. Finally they broke the ice higher up, crossed and started for a high mountain.

We sat down and ate the two biscuits which, with the greater part of a blue grouse, I had crowded into my pockets as we left camp. I sat down on the bank of the creek, produced my eatables, and I don't believe two hunters ever enjoyed a lunch more than we did this. By this time I was so exhausted that I began to feel as though I should fall by the side of the trail, but the hope that we would soon overtake the elks kept me stimulated to travel. We crossed a deep gorge, and started up a long mountain side, where the forest fires of last year had destroyed all of the beautiful green foliage, and had left only the charred bodies of the pines. But tender grasses had come again, however, with the spring, and we could see where the elks had eaten the sweet mosses as they toiled up the mountain.

Heavy perspiration was almost blinding me and I thought I had gone my full limit, when I heard the crash of a broken log and saw the whole band of elks charging through the timber to the west. Thinking nothing of fatigue and knowing they could not go straight up the rocks, we both started down the mountain like a pair of bloodhounds. Our time was short, if we were to capture our prize. On we went, falling over logs, tearing through the brush, until we reached the bottom. Our game had just crossed the stream, and was now in an open park.

Cal opened fire by sending a ball which threw up the dirt in front of the leader. This had the desired effect, turned the cow in her course, and, as she swerved down the hill, he sent another ball after her. Now was my time. I drew a full bead on her shoulder and fired, and she reeled down the hill like a drunken man. Our rifles banged in quick succession and the elks became bewildered. Cal got a shell stuck fast in his gun and was not a participant in the battle from that time.

We killed two large cows and wounded two bulls. We dressed the cows and were after the bulls, our course taking us through the worst jungle I have ever seen. Eventually we found where they had climbed up the broken rocks and fallen timber, until they had reached a situation where it was impossible for us either to get them out, or to take a horse where we could get at them at all.

The excitement was now over, our day's work was done and we were ten miles from camp. I cannot describe our return trip to camp, but we reached it about ten o'clock at

BAND OF ELK DURING MIDDAY.

On Ten Sleep River.

night, tired and bloody and famished. The elks fully filled out our load of game, making our trophies two elks and seven deer. We soon forgot how tired we were as the boys got us a good supper. Having secured our game, we started back to Buffalo and reached there two days later, after a delightful journey.

CHAPTER XXIX.

Our annual hunt for 1891 was looked forward to very eagerly and our plans were laid to start from Buffalo, Wyoming, early in October. The morning arrived and found us all on the move at an early hour. Cal Jennings, R. R. Woods, Ed. Chappell, Mr. Fender and myself comprised the party. Thoroughly equipped with two four-horse teams and saddle horses, we set out. We reached the mountain and found that snow was falling, making it doubly hard to climb, but we slowly ascended the almost perpendicular trail until until we reached the top, where we camped at an altitude of 8,570 feet. The first night was spent at the old Woodward sawmill, with the snow about two inches deep, and it was very cold.

Our first piece of bad luck was the death of Mr. Chappell's saddle-horse. The poor animal was sick only about two hours, the hard ride of the morning having brought on something like congestion of the lungs. We built a fire around him and gave him a pint of brandy, but he finally died without a struggle.

Our contemplated route lay over a country remarkable for its green pine forests interwoven with beautiful parks of wild bunch grass, some of them being miles in extent. As Mr. Jennings was best acquainted with the road, he took the lead, and Mr. Fender, an old hunter of Nebraska, followed with four as good cayuses as ever stretched a tug. Chappell rode Mr. Jennings' saddle mare, so our scouting party, Chappell, Woods and myself, were once more in the lead.

We kept up a lively pace until noon, when we camped on the banks of a beautiful little stream. After dinner our road turned off the main thoroughfare. We had not proceeded far on this when Mr. Woods and myself came upon two fresh lion-tracks which crossed the road. We dismounted, tied our horses, and, with our rifles, proceeded to hunt through the timber and rocks.

After we had made a circuit of several miles, the tracks of a third lion appeared. We came to a windfall about a mile square, and, through and around this terrible jungle, we circled three times, slipping and falling between logs repeatedly. The tracks crossed and recrossed until we became so confused that we could no longer follow them, and their chasings of rabbits made it all the more difficult. Having wasted five hours of toil, we were obliged to abandon the hunt.

After a long ride we found that our party had pulled out for Canyon creek. Just as we were crossing this branch, I saw five black-tail deer bounding toward us on a timber ridge. We halted and finally I could see that the rear one was wounded, so we knew that other hunters were in the field. At this point we made a curve and went back over the hill, bearing from south to north and, going in the direction of our party, followed them. When we came to the trail we separated, hoping by this means to cut off their retreat or get a running shot at them as they passed northward.

I went across a beautiful park and kept a sharp lookout for the deer, as I thought they would come my way. I had now reached a deep canyon and had dismounted to let my horse rest. Suddenly the clear report of Woods' rifle broke the stillness. Echoing and reechoing followed until the last sound rumbled along the mountain and died away. The sharp cry of an eagle made me turn my head in time to see the bird dash by like an arrow, but not a deer appeared. I kept on straining my eyes to see the glossy coats of deer gliding through the forest below me, but was continually doomed to disappointment, so I mounted my horse and started for camp.

Gaining the top of a mountain I could again see the summit of the mountain that I had named last year. Far beyond were the headwaters of Ten Sleep and Paint Rock. Hurriedly I pressed on until I gained the north side of the mountain, finding the snow so deep and cold that my horse could scarcely keep his feet. I dismounted and led the way, taking a course which I thought would bring me out at the Canyon Creek crossing. Hungry and tired I found the camp, but all the boys had gone hunting. I prepared supper and was doing some good work when Woods came in exhausted. He had not even a fawn to show for his interview with the band of deer.

The boys returned to camp, Cal coming in last, and I could see by the blood showing around his finger nails that he had killed something. He admitted having secured a couple of black-tail deer and we paid him the honor of making the first kill. We spent the night here, and, in the morning, while Cal and Mr. Fender went after the slain deer, the rest of us oiled the wagons, broke camp, and started for the middle branch of Lee Creek. After settling on a location for a camp, Woods, Chappell and I took our horses to see if we could also locate the elks for tomorrow's hunt. We set out on a brisk gallop, dashing over sagebrush, stones and numerous other obstacles. At the south of old

Baldy we agreed to separate, each one choosing his direction, planning to meet at Five Points, as our camp was just below that place.

After a weary climb, I came out upon a high woody divide which overlooked a tributary of Ten Sleep. Resting my horse, I rounded the steep rimrock, and started to cross a deep gorge in the mountains. The green hemlocks were thick, and the snow was deep, but not frozen on this side. Presently I crossed the trail made by thirty elks. They were headed straight for Ten Sleep canyon, the trail being at least three days old. I passed along and turned in the direction of Five Points, but was soon compelled to abandon the saddle, as the ground became too steep and rugged for horseback riding. Having failed in my attempt to cross the stream, I again started up the mountain and soon came upon another elk trail made by about fifteen cows and calves. They had forced a passage across and I followed. After carefully surveying all signs, I concluded the trail must have made the day before, so I turned away, after learning their direction, which I was certain was the same as that of the first band.

I was now gaining the second hill, which I was sure would lead me to Five Points. Here I soon found a fresh trail of seven elks that was going directly in the course that I was traveling, the trail evidently being not more than an hour old. As I pressed on and upward I was just about clear of the heavy timber, when a rifle shot rang out, followed by another and yet another, until nine successive shots had broken the stillness which had been so monotonous all day. Every moment I expected to see some old lead cow with expanded nostrils plunge through the forest on her back trail.

I mounted my horse and shot forward. I soon came

upon a cross trail, where the elks had plunged down the other side like an avalanche, falling over logs, jumping and plunging headlong. It was useless to follow them now, so I started for camp. When on the rimrock I caught sight of a cow as she sped past a small opening about three hundren yards away. I dashed after her at the top of my speed, urging Blackhawk at every bound. As I came to the precipice I saw three cows and a calf dash around the rimrock and disappear. But I rapidly followed, jumping ditches, logs and rocks until I gained the bottom, which opened into a park.

Here I saw a cow, which was among the rocks far up in the timber, turn and start back. Leaving my horse, I ran through the trees, keeping an open place in view, hoping that she would pass that way, but, instead of doing so, she turned again and took her first course, which would bring her out right at our camp. I remounted and followed as fast as I could until presently I found myself in a windfall so dense that it was impossible to proceed. Upon my return to camp I learned that our teamsters had seen the elk pass within five hundred yards. It was almost night, so we contented outselves by planning our program for the next day.

As this spot was to be our permanent camp, we earnestly set to work to make ourselves fully comfortable. Our large Sibley tent was soon set up in a beautiful little nook close to some evergreens, and we filled it a foot deep with hemlock, spruce and juniper boughs, the mingling of their odors giving out a delightful perfume. Every man worked with a will, and all preparations were speedily made. Then, after a supper of tenderloin venison, potatoes, onions, honey, biscuit, coffee and plums, we sat smoking the peace-pipe, and speculated on the location of the band of forty-five elks.

A sound sleep made us eager for the day's sport. Our horses were soon fed and saddled. After a splendid breakfast, we started up the divide. When we arrived at the top, we took different routes, but the whole day passed and we all came home empty-handed. Fender had seen two bears and had come across a new partner who was hunting in the mour'ains, and who stayed all night with us. The next day Mr. Woods made a splendid run, and, by a flank movement, bagged two black-tail deer, claiming second honors for this. The rest of the party had a hard day and accomplished nothing.

That evening I told Cal I believed our old camp would be a good place to visit, so we concluded to visit it and took that course and rode directly to the spring, to find that some forty head of elks had watered there. In the night we took the trail which led directly through the dense woods and deep snow toward the mountains. We carefully followed the trail for five or six miles, until we could see in the distance, a large south hillside with a dense growth of burnt timber. Cal said that the band of elks of which we were in pursuit might be lying on the south side sunning themselves, and that we must be very careful or we would not get a shot at them.

So as to make little noise, we tied our horses to the first trees, and proceeded up the mountain. As we were rounding a large slide of rocks I discovered that the trail divided, about half the number going to the right while the other half turned to the left. Cal was on my right and we were each straining every nerve, perspiring from every pore, when our elks broke cover. Cal's old Winchester spoke to one on the right just as I saw a handsome cow struggling to gain the top of the divide.

I threw myself down and fired at fully three hundred

yards. She reeled to the left and I fired again, a shot which stopped her. My new Bullard hissed a flame of fire, her neck cracked, and she dropped like a stone. Three balls had struck her, two of which would have been fatal. She was a barren young cow, and had a lovely skin, which I saved in honor of my new rifle. Cal now joined me, and we followed the band on their reckless stampede, but saw them no more. After taking out the entrails of the elk, we started for home, but struck other trails which we followed toward the main Paint Rock canyon.

After riding several miles, we came to the heavy trail of perhaps sixty elks. Farther along on our way we came to another trail of perhaps forty or fifty, all going in the same direction. Here we held a council of war, deciding at last to go home and return in the morning with our full force. On our homeward way, we encountered the most villainous route I ever traveled, and were compelled to surmount what seemed to be at first sight impassable barriers. Several times our horses fell over rocks and trees. I gave a sigh of relief when we approached camp and found all the other boys had arrived.

Chappell had got a shot at a deer, but so far off, and through such terrible brush, that the bullet was worn out before it reached the deer. Woods had crippled five or six of them and Fender had scared a doe into another territory. Cal and I then sprung our cow elk on them with the additional statement of seeing six or seven hundred more tracks, all of which we knew were not more than a mile from where we left them.

Early on the next morning we were in the saddle, our horses flying across the large parks, making a bee line toward where we had seen the trails the day before. Like a company of cavalrymen we went on until we found the trail. We followed this for six or eight miles and I could see that every fellow wanted to be in at the killing. As we approached a large body of timber on the south side, I proposed we get off and lead our horses, in order to go as carefully as possible, so that the elks would not see us first.

I went ahead, and slowly, until I could see that we were almost at the top. Here the band had scattered and were feeding leisurely along, cutting the tender vegetation and winding through every little park. I came to several large bull tracks and they seemed to be in the rear, which showed me very plainly that the rutting season was over, and the old cow had taken her position at the front. As we were now up the hill and were nearly exhausted from climbing, we mounted our horses and tried to ride very slowly. Woods was in the lead, I called the boys together and told them we were going too fast.

After going two hundred yards we came to where the herd had been lying down. Woods declared we had scared them and that the jig was up for today. After looking around we could see where some had been running, so I made a circle and saw that about forty elks had come into the main herd, and that this was the reason for their getting up at that time of day. I noticed by the hair on the trees in several places, that they had stopped there to rub themselves. We all advanced with eyes and ears open to catch the first object that moved. Woods was still ahead and on our right. Every one was doing his best to be noiseless and to move along as fast as he could.

To our right, fully one hundred yards ahead, the old Bullard carried by Woods startled us with a bang that made the mountains ring. With one mighty crash about a hundred and forty elks were tearing everything before them in their fright. Woods was the only man who got a shot. We all ran back after our horses and followed the running elk. They hurriedly fell, rolled and tumbled down the mountain. The trail was torn to atoms and the old rotten trees in their way were smashed and felled. It was absolutely the steepest trail I ever took a pony over. Cal made a crosscut on the band, intercepted them and got shots at two, both of which he hit. Woods gave chase to a large bull which he wounded.

Finally the band crossed the headwaters of the main Ten Sleep and started through a windfall. No horse could follow them there, so Cal left the trail and started for camp. We followed on Cal's trail and came to the spot where he had killed a fine black-tail deer. I warned the boys that we were now on a trail that they would long remember. We made a fair start, but had to dismount and drive our horses. Several times I thought they would break their necks by falling. I will not try to describe this trip, but merely say it was even worse than we had found it on the day before. We reached camp about nine o'clock and found Cal getting supper.

Early on the next morning, Fender, who was an old hunter and a fine shot, started with me after the cow elk with two ponies. We resolved to bring it in whole on a travoise, but for fear we might not succeed in this attempt, we took my 4x5 Hawkeye camera along, in order to at least get a photograph. When we neared the spot, our dog saw something run across a park and followed after it, but soon came back with his tail down. We saw by the size of its track that it was a huge mountain lion. I was afraid the elk had been torn to pieces, but the lion had only commenced to sample the kidney fat when we disturbed him.

While we pulled the cow down the hill, the magpies and the camp-robbers flew in every direction, seeking by their screams to scare us away. Our next move was to make a travoise. After carefully selecting two long tamarack saplings, we bound them together with ropes and attached a crosspiece on which to fasten the elk. Finally we were ready to start, and what a start it was. One pony was first hitched on, then two more ahead of him, but the animals utterly refused to pull such a load. At last we managed to set out, going over stones, trees, logs and brush, until we reached the bottom, where the load lodged against a big pine log. Over this log we could not get, so we had to give up our plan. To reach camp we had hundreds of worse places to cross.

After we had photographed the elk, we soon cut it up, packed the ponies and started for camp. Our delay had made us late, but when we got on top of the divide our pack horses were working well, and as we were nearing Five Points I took a snap-shot of them, just as the sun was dropping down over the mountains. We reached camp eventually and piled up our game, which comprised one elk and seven deer. Cal Jennings and Mr. Woods had killed the deer, and the elk was credited to me. This was the end of our Lee Creek hunt. The next day we pulled out for Canyon Creek crossing, where we camped.

While traveling toward the Canyon Creek we went ahead on the saddle horses and carefully hunted over some fine country, but failed to even make a score. When we reached Canyon Creek it was still early in the afternoon, so we decided to make one more effort for game. Mr. Woods, who had left us on account of urgent business, had lost the best part of the hunt, and all of us missed him. Jennings and Chappell left Fender and myself to pursue whatever course or direction we thought best, but, as there appeared to be no choice, we took the west side of the mountain while they took the east.

The farther we went, the thicker was the timber. The snow in many places was hard enough to hold our weight, but in many places there was no snow at all. I found a large buck and three doe tracks and trailed them until Mr. Fender got quite a distance ahead of me. The standing burned timber was so very thick I could scarcely get through it. The small poles, all as black as coal, stood up like straws in a field. We were keeping a sharp lookout for deer on every hand and I expected momently to see them bounding off.

We started toward the summit just as we heard Cal's Winchester bellowing, until nine shots had been fired. I kept a sharp lookout, for I felt sure that the game was coming our way. Presently a monstrous bull came directly toward Fender, and I could see two cows following at a distance of a hundred paces. The bull came rushing on with his head raised, smashing through the trees. The crash of Fender's gun started him westward, and down the mountain. The cows were gone too, although Fender fired at them, for no ball could get far through the trees.

I was sure the bull was unhurt, and, throwing my Bullard in line with his shoulder, I sent a hissing messenger after him. Quickly I shot again, and this time saw a handful of hair fly from his side. His back gave a downward hitch and I stopped, for I knew he was doomed. His great body swayed from side to side as he pressed on through the burned timber, striking his antlers, which were badly shattered from the many hard battles he had hitherto fought. He reeled about. The blood spurted from his side upon the trees. He tried to make one more effort to go on, but his knees trembled, and he fell headlong with a crash, and tumbled over against the trees. His eyes rolled in their sockets, his massive teeth ground together and he yielded up his life.

After taking out his entrails and cutting him up I found two bullets from Cal's rifle in his carcass. Cal had made a lucky shot through the timber and had killed a cow. We now had all the meat we could haul. After a hard evening's work we got to camp about nine o'clock, tired out. Our hunt was now over. The busy life of the world again called us to resume its activities. Therefore early on the next morning we packed up the belongings of our camp and started for Buffalo. Our teams were loaded to their full capacity. Upon our arrival at our home we were welcomed by a host of friends whom we loaded down with elk and deer meat. The next morning we parted as hunters until September, 1892, when we all agreed to meet and join in the excitements and the pleasures of the chase again.

CHAPTER XXX.

OUR BROTHERS OF THE FOREST—Lost to the outside world—birds—red deer—animal speech—gray wolf—elk—ruffed grouse—a splendid specimen.

As we penetrate the massive openings of the great forests of the Rocky Mountains, whose towering pines stand like sentinels, we are completely lost persons to the outside world. In these forests nature is most beautiful and wonderful and prodigal. Here unite the soft love-notes of birds, wooing their mates, the chattering of the "camp-robber," Both commingle with the "who, who," of the cat owl, loftily perched in the top of a pine. Down upon this denizen of the night presently a great bald eagle makes a swoop, startling the owl from his meditations. The cry of the eagle, thrown out as the owl escapes down the canyon, is taken up by the crows who give battle to the owl. The echoes multiply, sink away, rise again, and finally die away to utter silence.

In this grand canyon, where we are now reposing, which is covered by a foliage so dense that the sun's rays have never penetrated the dark recesses of the shady nooks, we are not alone. The limbs of the ancient trees are robed with moss of a greenish-gray tint. As silently as shadows, we see a family of red deer (cervus Virginianus) pass rapidly along over the carpet of pine needles centuries old. Noiselessly each one stoops down to take a tuft of rich bunch grass. Then the head, with ears thrown forward, is raised to detect the faintest sound, the beauiful brown eyes scanning every bush and tree. Now come the fawns, bounding with delight, scarcely ruffling a bough in their progress.

Suddenly a cry falls on their ears like a death knell. Their blood is frozen in their veins by fear, as again that low, plaintive wail smites their ears. The hunter, too, well understands this baneful sound. It is the female cougar (felis concolor) calling her lord to join her in the chase for blood. The fawns even understand the cry, and trembling, huddle against their elders.

The mother, who is always prepared for the worst, runs to a thicket of bushes, and, with a low warning appeal to her loved ones, who always understand, secretes herself. When the youngsters are hidden, and are as still as statues, the parents bound away in an opposite direction to decoy the dreaded enemy from the neighborhood of their young. The cougars follow them as rapidly as possible. When they are thus drawn far away from the hiding place of their offspring, the deer increase their speed and the cougars are left discomfited at a safe distance from the fawns, whose parents return to them by a circuitous route.

It is my opinion that all animals have power of audible speech. Their vocabulary may not be extensive, but it answers the purpose. When a storm is gathering, the large gray wolf (canis occidentalis) of the plains goes to a high point and utters a dismal, prolonged howl, which is soon answered by all the wolves within his hearing. He is calling his band together to pull down a horse, steer, or other larger game, that all may have food before the storm breaks. The horses and cows of the plains well know what the direful cry means, and bound away at highest speed as soon as they hear the call for blood.

The mother antelope with one word secretes her off-

spring under a sagebush, believing it to be safe when it is
out of sight, and rushes away. When the danger is removed, she returns, and one call brings it forth. All young
animals are obedient to the mother's call, for there is no
false word or note in the language of animals.

When the hunter has been stalking a band of elks for
miles through the dense forest, and, being at some distance behind them, finds eventually that they have lain
down, he always discovers that the old cow leader is in a
position to look backward along the trail. The instant this
ever-faithful leader detects the approach of a hunter, she
gives a sharp whistle as a danger signal, and the entire band
at once bounds away from the intruder. None wait, even
an instant, to see if it be a false alarm, for there is never
any doubt, uncertainly or deception.

The American ruffed grouse has probably been more
discussed than any other bird of the west. The grouse is
always a favorite bird with the sportsman, and its habits
are governed largely by existing circumstances. With the
eye of an eagle, the cunning of a fox, the carriage of a
queen, the plumage of a peacock, it has the boldness of a
lion. It is a wild adventurer who unconcernedly penetrates
the deepest forest, and depends upon the unbroken wilderness for its daily bread. This grouse is an inveterate wan-
derer, for I have seen him in Pennsylvania, Ohio, Illinois,
Wisconsin, Dakota, Wyoming and Montana.

I have watched a male stand on his tiptoes upon an old
log, and, with an inflated breast, upon which he beats with
his wings, begin to play the long roll, thumping faster and
faster, until the vibrations sounded like a long roll of drums.
Some sportsmen contend that the grouse beats upon the log
with his wings to make the sound. I have, however, carefully watched him with a field glass from a distance of sixty

yards, and have seen him expand his chest, as does the athlete, and thus make his drum, for the calls which set the forest in a whirl, and notifies his sweetheart of his presence.

How to kill the ruffed grouse is a topic upon which every sportsman has an opinion. When I was a boy I used to go into the Ohio beech woods with a little, coarse-haired terrier and wait until I heard him bark. Then I began to whistle, for I thought that under the then existing circumstances, the grouse would take no notice of me. Invariably, I found this beautiful bird intently watching the dog that bounded about him, barking. I soon found that my whistling counted for nothing, and a careful shot always landed my prize under the tree.

In Montana they present a much darker color than that of the eastern birds. At the sight of a dog they will fly quickly into a small tree and sit perfectly still, while you walk all around them among the low trees. Once, when returning to camp, after a vain search for a bear, I struck a thicket of cottonwoods and quaking-asps, so dense that I was compelled to crawl through it on my knees. Suddenly, I heard the quick whirr of a grouse's flight, and the bird perched himself on a limb that was clearly outlined in the moonlight. I had his whole body silhouetted and it was a beautiful picture. The crest of feathers upon his head shown as plainly as though the time were midday. I drew a bead for his neck and fired. His plump body fell like a stone, and I still preserve his stuffed skin as a memento of the grouse seen and killed in my boyhood days, although he differs from them in color.

To the student of animal life and of animal history, a hunter's sojourn in the primitive Rockies was a continual delight. Every day brought something new. Every tramp after game, when one's eyes and senses were preternaturally active, was almost a new revelation. The children of the wild were there seen in all of their moods and revealed themselves as they really are. No stuffed bird or beast in a museum is to be ever compared with the animal in its native state and home. I have been highly favored in this respect.

CHAPTER XXXI.

CONCLUSION.

Those days are gone and my retrospect is now ended.
"Ye have lived my life, ye have heard my tale," and I must
say farewell. And yet I linger. The new days are so unlike
the old. The free, wild life of nature and of nature studies
has been so changed by the circumscribing influence of civilization, so measured by metes and bounds, that we are now
living the life of another world. I cling to the memories of
the past with the warmth and tenacity of the ardent lover,
and the reader will bear me if I indulge in a closing remi-
niscence. I can still see, by the clear mountain streams, the
busy beavers of the olden time, cutting trees and building
dams to provide the water in which they can build their
houses and be protected from the intrusions of their brothers
of the wild. By their extermination one large element of the
purchasing power of the Indian has passed away. All
things of that loved period have passed.

Link after link has dropped off from the chain of primitive existence. The deer have been killed, their skins taken
to the East and made into gloves, while the remnants of the
once great tribes of Indians must now resort to other means
to secure their footwear. Their moccasined feet no longer
sound noiselessly on plain and mountain. The juicy venison is no longer an article of staple food. The agile red and

black-tailed deer no longer bound in bands along the water-
courses or over the plains and hills. The enormous herds
of elk, whose tread once shook the earth as their massive
forms thundered down the mountain side or dashed across
the valleys, have disappeared.

The dusky warrior no longer rides his war-horse, in
feathered pride of painted war array, across the plains, or
sends his obsidian arrow hurtling through the heart of elk
or buffalo. No longer the braves meet in battle, bedecked
in war paint, for the extermination of other tribes, or to
swoop down on pioneer settlements with their blood-curdling
yells and flashing hatchets. No longer the Indian lover brings
the trophies of the chase to the tepee door of his brown-
eyed betrothed. No longer is their summer home pitched
amid the profusion of wild flowers, the sweet perfumed
cedars and pines. Thousand of such tepees once dotted the
plains, the benches, and the margins of the streams, where
the inmates passed their wild life as happy in their childish
enjoyments as the day was long. Here, too, they danced the
war-dance, where frenzied braves kept time to the weird
monotonous music of the tomtom, the flickering light of
the camp-fires rendered aromatic by the red willow and
kinni-kinnick plentifully supplied as fuel, which cast a yellow radiance over the infernal conclave, making the glittering
forms of the eagle-plumed warriors, as they trod the meas-
ures of the dance, appear like devils just issuing from the
gates of hell. All, all, are gone. The happy life and the
evil life are now things of the past, soon to be unknown,
even in memory, to the people of the land.

I must say farewell to all of these, and to the buffalo,
whose countless droves were in number as the trees of the
forest, stretching in almost one unbroken mass from the
Staked Plains to the Canadian line. They furnished lodges

and meat for the hordes of Indians dwelling on the plains. Their robes were downy blankets, and could be exchanged for ammunition, knives, beads, and for the gaudily woven blankets of the white man. Their sinews formed the bow-strings that whizzed the deadly arrows to the living mark of animals or men. They were watched and guarded as the white man guards and watches his costliest herds. All gone, all gone, they are now things of the past. All of the wild life and all of its wild nature has passed from the earth. To them all I here say farewell. And farewell to the grand old Rockies.

"Farewell to the Rockies," did I say? Never. They yet exist; and to them I shall never say farewell, until my eye-lids, glazed by death, refuse me their sight. The grand old Rockies! with their snow-clad peaks, whose tops are lost in the immensity of Heaven's own blue, where wind and storm and snow, glaciers and waterfalls abound, where Indian history and mythology are carved in imperishable records on granite walls, where yet stands the sheep-eater's pile of bones. To them I will not say farewell. Eternal in their existence, the backbone of the American continent, they will ever divide the waters of the Atlantic and the Pacific. They will still hoard up for the use of coming men the hidden treasures, now concealed for uncounted centuries, treasures of shining sapphires, rubies, amethysts, gold, much gold, and silver, and copper, and iron. They will still send forth the crystal streams of pure, life-giving water for the delec-tation and refreshment of man, and that the whole land may be carpeted with richest grasses, ornamented with flowers of wondrous beauty, provided with a giant growth of pine, hemlock, cedar, fir, aspen, willow and cottonwood. The liquid streams will ever spring from solid ice fountains deep down in the thousand massive glaciers of everlasting brilliancy, sparkling like morning dew in the glint of the sunshine.

Grand old Rockies! Thy beauties no artist can ever portray. Thy charms no poet's pen describe. To you I can never say farewell, and, when my spirit takes its flight to the great God who has permitted me to tarry so long in this delightful region, may I be permitted to pass away with my eyes resting upon thy unequaled magnificence and beauty when the evening sun casts its last declining rays on the gold and scarlet, jasper and emerald coloring presented on your gorgeous, towering and familiar peaks.